THE CONVERT

AND THE COUNSELLOR

THE DISCIPLES CHECKLIST

Okey Onuzo

The Convert and the Counsellor... The Disciple's Checklist

First Edition 1990

Second Edition 2011

Third Edition 2020

ISBN: 978-1-880608-13-5

THIRD REVISED EDITION

Published by,

Life Link Worldwide Publishers

175 Raymond Court, Fayetteville GA 30214 USA

For more information and book orders visit amazon.com and amazon.co.uk

TABLE OF CONTENTS

PREAMBLE

On June 28th, 1970, I attended a meeting in Enugu, organized by the Scripture Union Group. I went there merely to find out for myself what they had to say about being born again. It was my younger sister Ngo that introduced the term to me.

At the end of that meeting, or rather before I finally left that meeting venue, I had signed a piece of paper to indicate that I had given my life to Christ. That meant I was born again. Nobody told me in that meeting what was supposed to have happened to me. Nobody explained in any detail what to expect. That would be too much to ask of a preacher in a thirty to a forty-five-minute sermon. The good Lord touched my heart and drew me to Himself. That was what happened on the day that I was born again.

As a lay-minister of God over the years, one of the most significant problems that I have encountered is how to ensure that all those who answer the "altar call" to give their hearts to Jesus are adequately followed-up so they could follow Christ with understanding. There is a need to be rooted and grounded in God's love and the truth in God's Word. A professional colleague of mine, also a lay-minister of God, told me of a young lady soliciting one of the highways in a particular city in Nigeria. The gentleman that she approached declined her overtures and explained to her that as a born-again child of God, he could not indulge in such affairs anymore. The lady shocked him by saying that she was born again; her reason was that circumstances beyond her control forced her to take to the streets.

Follow up is a primary duty of Christians. This book does not eliminate those house calls that are so useful in confirming the faith of the young convert to Christ. It is not to make us all sit home and simply pray that they will use the book. It will never replace those calls where we share from the depths of our hearts how we came to love the Lord so much so that nothing else has mattered that much ever since. It is there that we dare to confide that things were not always this way with us. We stop to open our hearts to share with our young convert, our struggles and our victories, and the times we had failed. Nothing can replace those person-to-person interactions that mean so much to the young convert to Christ, who is eager to learn.

I believe what the Holy Ghost wants me to do here is see if, by His grace, I can be used to produce what you can leave behind with the young believer. Something additional to that crucial visit: Something he or she can refer to for consolidation after you have gone: Some kind of reference support.

There is no way a book like this can be exhaustive. It is not supposed to be. My prayer is that it will serve its intended purpose, which is to help the young believer in Christ go through the early days of his or her newfound faith in God through Christ

Sources of Bible quotations

CSB – Christian Standard Bible

GNB - Good News Bible

KJV - King James Version

NIV - New International Version

NLT2 – New Living Translation

NKJV - New King James Version

NRSV –New Revised Standard Version

TEV – Todays English Version

TLB –The Living Bible

PREFACE
TO THE THIRD EDITION

12And from the days of John the Baptist until now the kingdom of heaven suffereth violence, and the violent take it by force.

- (Matthew 11:12 (KJV)

The Kingdom of God suffers violence, and the violent take it by force. When this book was first published in 1990, it was inspired by the desire to consolidate the faith of the many new believers who were being saved in the mini-revival in the mid-eighties. It was also to help raise enough counsellors to take up that irreplaceable task of visiting new converts to establish their newfound faith in Christ Jesus, our Lord, and Savior.

Now, what we have are Churches that are full but with believers that have a poor grasp or no grasp of fundamental Christianity. Although we admit that our world is changing in many respects, we must equally acknowledge that the Kingdom of God and its requirements have not changed. Yes, so many things have changed around us since 1990 some thirty years ago when the first edition was released. Technology has changed. The mobile phone has exploded in every nation, and God's Word has become more accessible as a result. iPads, iPods, laptops have all contributed to making access to God's Word well within reach of many, if not all.

Now and again, we have new members join our family either as workers or as family friends. We discover that the level of knowledge they have of their faith in Christ has reduced considerably. In our nation Nigeria, the Churches are still full. The numbers are still impressive, but the level of knowledge has gone down. Soon after the first edition was released, a new convert was given a free copy at the Full Gospel Business Men's Fellowship International meeting. About four weeks later, he invited me to speak at the discipleship class he organized in his Church. He told me that he read the book three times and then started a discipleship group of his own. Through studying 'The Convert and the Counsellor', he was able to go from convert to counsellor in just four weeks.

For the past thirty months and counting, we have been praying for the Holy Spirit's outpouring in yet another move of God. But this time around, we are hoping for a global dimension, for we believe that we are at the threshold of a mighty and fresh outpouring of the Spirit of God. This third edition has been prepared with that objective in mind; to raise a huge number of disciples who will arise to consolidate the faith of many new and not so new believers and send them marching confidently to reap the harvest of these end-times. By adding the subtitle, THE DISCIPLE'S CHECKLIST, this third edition is more comprehensive as details have been added to assist a believer plant his two feet firmly on the road that is straight and narrow.

My prayer is that the Holy Spirit will use this 3rd edition more than He used the earlier two to establish the Kingdom of God in the hearts of men and women in Jesus' name, Amen.

Okey Onuzo

Convener

Kingdom Life Seminar

Your Fellow Pilgrim

NOTE: The following chapters capture a new convert's conversations with a mature believer in Christ. The mature Christian, his counsellor, attempts to answer his questions regarding his new faith. The convert's questions are highlighted in bold text while the counsellor's responses follow in plain text.

1.

UNDERSTANDING THE NEW BIRTH EXPERIENCE

***

What does it mean to be born again?

Our Lord Jesus Christ used the phrase *born again* in His discussions with the Jewish leader, Nicodemus. You may find this in the Gospel of John chapter 3, from verses 1 to 7. I think you should get your Bible and read the passage. What may strike you there is the emphasis, particularly in verses 3, 5, and 7:

"Jesus answered and said unto him, Verily, verily, I say unto thee, Except a man be born again, he cannot see the kingdom of God." (KJV)

He repeatedly emphasized that an individual must be born again. You can see that what you have just done is something that Jesus says you just must-do if you want to enter the Kingdom of God. So, you might say that the new birth is the gateway to the Kingdom of God. Let us put it this way: A person coming into this world must be born into it. There is no other way to go in. Similarly, a person entering into the Kingdom of God is born into it. There is just no other way to go in.

Can you make it simpler?

The best way to answer that question is to look closely at verse 6 of John chapter 3.

"That which is born of the flesh is flesh, and that which is born of the Spirit is spirit."

This passage implies that an individual undergoes two kinds of birth. One is physical; the other is spiritual. The physical precedes the spiritual. I suppose what one should ask is what it means to be born spiritually. To answer that question correctly, I believe we should touch on fundamental issues relating to a man's relationship with God. Two of these are quite remarkable. The first is the nature of man; the second is the fall of man. Let us take them one by one.

i. The Nature of Man

We gained some useful insight into the nature of man from Genesis chapter 2 and verse 7 when the Almighty God created him.

"And the Lord God formed man of the dust of the ground and breathed into his nostrils the breath of life, and man became a living soul."

When the Bible says that God formed man out of the dust of the earth, I believe it refers to human anatomy, which we can call structure and human physiology and biochemistry, which relates to his body's function. Simply put, man is very close to nature because the human body contains the same minerals found in the soil around us. Now we can understand why a man's body decays after death and returns to dust again, providing food for plants and other types of living things.

After God formed the body from the minerals in the soil, that body had no life in it until the Spirit of God referred to here as God's breath of life, entered it. When the life-giving Spirit of God, touched that lifeless body, the man became conscious or aware. The Bible says he started from the moment of that contact to have a soul. So we may conclude that a man has three parts to him: his body, his soul, and his spirit.

There are quite a few people who find it difficult to tell the difference between the soul and the spirit of man. The way to understand it is to separate them into three parts, according to their origins. The body came from the earth. The human spirit came from God. The soul is the result of the Spirit of God's impact on the man's lifeless body. It exists as human consciousness, and it manifests in three key areas: the will, the intellect, and the emotion. It is essential to bear the nature of man in mind because it helps us understand man's fall or what we call his 'original sin.'

ii. The Fall of Man

The LORD God Almighty wanted the man He created to be in charge of the earth. He made this clear to Adam and his wife in Genesis 1:28.

"And God blessed them, and God said unto them. Be fruitful, and multiply, and replenish the earth, and subdue it: and have dominion over the fish of the sea, and over the fowl of the air, and over every living thing that moveth upon the earth." [KJV]

Because the man was in charge on God's behalf, He made a covenant with him, a kind of contract or agreement. He put the man and his wife in the Garden of Eden. He made a covenant with them, which says that God is truly the one in charge; man is only in charge on God's behalf. The garden had a tree, which symbolized the agreement God made with the man. It was called the *Tree of the Knowledge of Good and Evil*. The man was not to determine good and evil by himself. Things should be good or evil, depending on how God had labeled them. The LORD put it to the man in Genesis 2:16-17.

"And the Lord God commanded the man, saying, Of every tree of the garden thou mayest freely eat:

But of the tree of the knowledge of good and evil, thou shalt not eat of it: for in the day that thou eatest thereof thou shalt surely die." [KJV]

The key to understanding the fall of man is in that statement that denotes the consequences of failure to comply: "thou shall surely die."

You may need to read Genesis 3:1-19 to get the whole picture. To cut a long story short: The devil convinced the man and his wife to eat fruit from this tree. Consequent to this disobedience, they died, but not physically. They died spiritually by losing the indwelling presence of the Spirit of God. Their human spirit lost its online connection with the Spirit of God.

When Jesus our Lord referred to spiritual birth in John chapter 3, as the gateway into the Kingdom of God, He meant that the Spirit of God must return to dwell in anyone who seeks to share eternity with Almighty God. It is important to note that when the Spirit of God departed from man, thereby disconnecting the spirit in man from the Spirit of God, the man began to live according to his soul's dictates. What this means practically is that man started to act, not as God wills any longer, but according to the way he wants, thinks, or feels. I am sure you can identify with that in your everyday life. I certainly can.

Let us conclude by saying that what happens when a person is born again is that the Spirit of God comes into him, quickens his human spirit and dwells with him. This quickened human spirit enables the individual to communicate with the Spirit of God now dwelling within him. This direct exchange also empowers the man to know God's mind and do His will on the earth.

Please explain the new birth process again.

I think it is helpful to know some of the consequences of man's fall as this helps explain the new birth process. The one key thing that happened at the fall of man is that he acquired the nature to sin when he disobeyed God Almighty in the Garden of Eden. The sin nature is this tendency we all have within us to choose evil rather than good. You may define evil as a combination of thoughts and actions outside of what God has said or commanded. The Bible recorded in Genesis chapter 6 that the ideas and imaginations of man's heart became evil continually after the fall. This is not too difficult to understand, for we all have to struggle to do what is right while doing what is wrong always appears more natural. We can see this in the Bible in Romans, Chapter 3 and verse 23, where it says:

"For all have sinned, and come short of the glory of God." [KJV]

The Wages of Sin

God has a law concerning sin. That law is stated clearly in Ezekiel chapter 18, verse 4. It is also in Romans chapter 6 and verse 23. You may check these out now, but here is what they say:

4*"Behold, all souls are Mine; The soul of the father, As well as the soul of the son is Mine; The soul who sins shall die.*

- Ezekiel 18:4 [NKJV]

"For the wages of sin is death..." (Romans 6:23a KJV)

You will agree that if God were to carry out this law to the letter, there would be nobody alive on earth. So what God did was to provide man with a substitute. You may read about all these in the Bible - 'Leviticus,' mainly chapters 3, 5, 6, 7, and 17.

There are two types of offerings prescribed. One is the peace offering when a man seeks reconciliation with God, and the other is the trespass offering or the sin offering.

With the peace offering, a man brings the substitute animal and lays his hand on the animal's head, before the priest offers it as a sacrifice on the altar. The blood of that animal poured on the altar symbolizes the life given to atone for sin.

With the sin or trespass offering, a person brings the animal again to the priest who kills it and makes atonement or provides a covering for his sin.

You can see immediately that this can be quite tedious and cumbersome. Besides, the people soon allowed the whole thing to degenerate into a ritual. Rather than provide them with a point of contact with God or drive them to holy living, it became appeasement. What happened is that they would live just the way they liked, but still maintain the sacrifices.

When God saw this, He changed the rules of reconciliation. He now set out to provide the sacrifice by Himself in the death of Jesus Christ. Besides, He required the believer in God through Christ to conform to the lifestyle of His Son, Jesus Christ. Let's take a look at Romans 8:29-30:(TEV)

29 Those whom God had already chosen he also set apart to become like his Son, so that the Son would be the first among many believers.

30 And so those whom God set apart, he called; and those he called, he put right with himself, and he shared his glory with them.

This is the love of God revealed in John 3:16.

"For God so loved the world that he gave his only begotten Son, that whosoever believeth in him should not perish, but have everlasting life." (John 3:16 KJV)

When you answered that 'altar call,' what you did was:

- Agree with God that you are a sinner who deserves to die.
- Ask for His forgiveness and seek reconciliation with Him by accepting to quit a life of sin. We call this repentance.
- Accept that the death of Jesus on the Cross of Calvary was your substitute sacrifice for your many sins.

- Accept that because Jesus died in your place, you should now live His life: And the only way to do this effectively is by allowing Him to become your personal Lord and Saviour. That way He can live His life through you by the quickening power of the Holy Spirit.

Repentance

Please tell me more about repentance.

When it comes to repentance, one helpful thing is to remember that there are four parts to it.

1. Sorrow for sin

One must be sorry for his sins. It is impossible to enjoy sinning and still claim to have repented. The Bible calls it godly sorrow in 2nd Corinthians 7:9-10.

9 Now I am glad I sent it, not because it hurt you, but because the pain caused you to repent and change your ways. It was the kind of sorrow God wants his people to have, so you were not harmed by us in any way.

10 For the kind of sorrow, God wants us to experience leads us away from sin and results in salvation. There's no regret for that kind of sorrow. But worldly sorrow, which lacks repentance, results in spiritual death. (2 Corinthians 7:9-10 (NLT2)

2. The Plea for God's Mercy and Forgiveness

It is important to remember this because some people do not believe that a person can be forgiven for his sins. They teach that one must pay the full penalty for his sins. Indeed, one should pay a full penalty for his or her sins. But if someone has paid for you, then you can be forgiven. The psalmist echoed this when he says that the man whose sins are forgiven, is truly blessed. You may find this in Psalm 32. Forgiveness is, therefore, an act of grace, the grace of God.

3. Asking God for Cleansing in the Blood of Jesus

Some people wonder why we should ask for cleansing from all our sins in the blood of Jesus. Some wonder why we should not just ask for forgiveness.

The reason lies in what we had shared earlier. The wages of sin is and will always remain death. Therefore, each time a person asks for cleansing in the blood of Jesus, he pays the full penalty for sin, by substitution, which the righteousness and the holiness of God Almighty demand, - the death of Christ for my sins.

4. Quitting a life of Sin

The fourth step is to ask for God's help not to go back to your sins again. Without this fourth part, repentance cannot be complete. This is because God's forgiveness through the sacrificial death of Jesus Christ is not to provide men with the licence to sin: instead, it provides a gateway to escape from the bondage of sin. You may notice that the Apostle Paul speaking by the Holy Spirit was concerned about this, in his letter to the Romans chapter 6, verse 1, where he asked: *"Are we to remain in sin so that God's grace (favour and mercy) may multiply and overflow? Certainly not! How can we who died to sin live in it any longer?"* [Amp. Bible] But more on this later.

GRACE

I do hear a great deal about grace.

Yes, because grace is at the centre of what God has provided for man through Christ Jesus. It means unmerited favour. There is a passage in the Bible that helps us to appreciate this very well.

"For scarcely for a righteous man will one die; yet perhaps for a good man someone would even dare to die. But God demonstrates His own love towards us, in that while we were still sinners, Christ died for us."

(Romans 5:7, 8 NKJV)

Another passage is quite helpful.

"For it is by grace that you have been saved, through faith and this is not from yourselves, it is the gift of God not by works, so that no one can boast." [Ephesians 2:8, 9 NIV]

An appreciation of the depth of God's grace in Christ Jesus does create in us a deep sense of gratitude and commitment to Him. Our Lord Jesus stated this when he said that the individual who has been forgiven much, loves much. [Luke 7:47]

I believe the Apostle Paul spoke for all of us when he said in Romans chapter 7 from verse 18:

"For I know that in me (that is, in my flesh) nothing good dwells; for to will is present with me, but how to perform what is good I do not find. For the good that I will, to do, I do not do; but the evil I will, not to do, that I practice." [Romans 7:18, 19 NKJV]

Anybody who has tried making a new year resolution can identify with that sort of frustration. But despite that kind of repeated failure, God still stepped in to make provision for our salvation. That is the meaning of God's grace in Christ Jesus. God's grace is about God's love and patience with the sinner, giving him time to repent of his sins.

THE LORDSHIP OF JESUS

What does it mean to make Jesus the Lord of my life?

I am glad you raised this question because it is really at the heart of any meaningful Christian life. I believe the first thing we need to appreciate is the basis of accepting Jesus Christ as one's personal Lord and Saviour. Why should you, for instance, accept Jesus as your Lord and Saviour? It bothers on exchange.

And what do you mean by that?

If someone died so that you may live, it is not that difficult to accept that person as Saviour. It is only a matter of gratitude. Here is how the Bible explains the exchange:

14 We are ruled by the love of Christ, now that we recognize that one man died for everyone, which means that they all share in his death.

15 He died for all, so that those who live should no longer live for themselves, but only for him who died and was raised to life for their sake.

If He died the death that we should have died, then we are honour bound if not duty-bound to try as much as possible to live the life He should have lived. This is the meaning of the exchange I spoke about earlier.

- 2 Corinthians 5:14-15 (TEV)

I suppose that follows naturally. But this concept of dying to multiply oneself sounds quite strange. Human beings, by our nature, are not accustomed to that kind of thinking. It is too much of a sacrifice to ask of anybody.

That is quite true. It is a concept that our Lord Jesus taught, borrowing from the process of multiplication in plant biology, or farming, or agriculture if you please. The setting in which He taught that principle is unique. It was at one of these great feast festivals in Jerusalem when there usually was a large gathering of visitors to the city. Many of them obviously must have heard quite a great deal about this itinerant evangelist from Nazareth, who demonstrated power and authority over every conceivable thing, from diseases to evil spirits to winds and waves, even to death. So naturally, a great many of them thought it was worth their while to meet Jesus.

The Bible recorded this incident in John, chapter 12.

"Some Greeks who had come to Jerusalem to attend the Passover paid a visit to Philip, who was from Bethsaida and said. Sir, we want to meet Jesus. Philip told Andrew about it, and they went together to ask Jesus. Jesus replied that the time had come for Him to return to His glory in heaven and that I must fall and die like a kernel of wheat that falls into the furrows of the earth. Unless I die, I will be alone - a single seed. But my death will produce many wheat kernels - a plentiful harvest of new lives'..." [John 12:20-24 TLB]

What fascinates me about this story is that our Lord Jesus had a clear idea of His earthly mission and was not ready to be carried away by the enormous popularity that followed His teachings and miracles. It is a level of detachment that is most impressive. I am sure you do appreciate what I mean.

Oh, yes, I certainly do. Not getting swollen headed in the middle of such a great success, is a tremendous accomplishment.

Oh, it certainly is. Through this, He borrowed from nature, noting that there is life through death. It is deep and real, for it is by His sacrifice, which reflects His love, that His gospel of love and man's reconciliation with God is still changing lives today almost two thousand years after His departure. But let us talk a little bit about how one can appreciate the Lordship of Jesus in his or her life. I suppose the idea of a Lord is not altogether a strange one. A cursory glance at the set up in feudal oligarchies will prove quite instructive.

There is a story or, in fact, two stories in the Bible that help a great deal. I recall that once I recast one of them in a modem setting, some in my audience were not amused.

Which story is that?

It is that one on the triumphal entry of our Lord Jesus into Jerusalem, which we celebrate as Palm Sunday.

How did you put it?

There was this bit about the fellows who owned the donkey or colt that Jesus rode on.

I think I remember that from my Sunday School days.

Ok, let us just look at the account of it in Mark's Gospel.

"As they approached Jerusalem and came to Bethphage and Bethany at the Mount of Olives, Jesus sent two of His disciples, saying to them, Go to the village ahead of you, and just as you enter it, you will find a colt tied there, which no one has ever ridden. Untie it and bring it here. If anyone asks you, 'Why are you doing this?' tell him, The Lord needs it..." [Mark 11:1-3 NIV]

As a story, it makes some interesting reading until you begin to analyze the implications of it. You know the colt was the prized means of transportation at the time. So, a new colt would be something like a brand-new car that you have just bought, which you have never driven. Say you have just bought yourself a brand-new Mercedes or Cadillac or BMW or a Rolls Royce. It's parked on your driveway or in front of your house. A total stranger comes and, without a word, begins to fiddle with the ignition to start the car. Then you bark out: "What on earth do you think you are doing?" They turn around and look up and say to you: "Oh, sorry, we didn't know you were around. The LORD needs this car now. He said just to tell you that."

Then you turn around and say: "Ok! It's Ok, if the LORD needs it. You can go ahead."

I can tell you for sure, that is a tough one.

It certainly is. But that is what it means to accept Jesus as Lord. If the Lord needs it, then let Him have it. If the Lord says drop it, then you lose it. If He says: "let go," then you let go. You simply do what He says.

The second story is quite similar in a sense. It was this matter about turning water into wine at the marriage feast in Cana in Galilee, as recorded in John chapter two. The mother of Jesus had instructed the servants carefully with these words: "Whatsoever He asks you to do, do it."

Now you can see that it is a tough one too. And by the way, what Jesus asked them to do wouldn't have made much sense to them or to any of us. The problem was that the wine had run out. Jesus asked the servants to go and start fetching water. After they had filled the pots, He asked them to serve the water to the guests. I don't know anybody who wouldn't wonder what the gentleman was up to some form of a joke or something. But the important thing is that when they obeyed, it worked; it solved the problem.

My, oh my! That, too, is a tough one. It worked anyway. It didn't make sense to them, but it worked. I need to remember that.

We all do. Sometimes we think we have figured it all out. But then when we ask the Lord, sometimes He tells us something we feel is way out. But if we obey it, we find it works; and that is the bottom line. I must always remind myself to test the power of obedience.

I think I am beginning to appreciate how this Lordship is supposed to work.

I am glad you are.

2.

WHAT IS NEXT?

Now that I am born again, what is next? I am not quite sure.

The Need for Change

Let me answer that with a song whose lyrics speak about the way forward:

Things are different now; something happened to me
When I gave my life to Jesus
Things are different now; something happened to me
When I gave my life to Him.
Things I loved before are passed away
Things I love far more, have come to stay

Things are different now; something happened to me
When I gave my life to Him. [Author unknown]

This song derives from a passage in the Bible,
which you will find in 2nd Corinthians 5:17. The
Amplified Bible puts it this way:

"Therefore, if anyone is in Christ, he is a new creation;
old things have passed away; behold all things have
become new."

This passage implies that once a person
becomes a born-again Christian, they should be
able to see a difference in their lives. There would
be old lifestyles, old habits, old ways, and old
thought patterns that would be incompatible with
their new life, which they would readily exchange
for God's new ways of doing things. The apostle
James implied in his letter in James 2, from verse
14, that if this change or result of the new-found
faith is not manifest, then the new life itself does
not exist.

How does this change come about?

For us to experience this change, our thoughts and thought patterns will require some restructuring. The Bible puts it this way in Romans 12:2 (ISV):

Stop being conformed to this world, but continue to be transformed by the renewing of your minds so that you may be able to determine what is God's will — what is proper, pleasing, and perfect.

The primary instrument of change is the Word of God, the Bible. You should study it for yourself, have it explained to you by others, and discuss your understanding of it in fellowship with others to enhance your grasp of what it reveals about God, man, and life. Listen to what it says about its purpose:

"All Scripture is given by inspiration of God, and is profitable for doctrine, for reproof, for correction, for instruction in righteousness, that the man of God may

be complete, thoroughly equipped for every good work."
[2nd Timothy 3:16,17 NKJV]

I would like you to give some examples.

Some passages detail some of the fundamental changes that should take place. I will outline a few of them here and then list a good many others for you to check for yourself.

16 So I say, live by the Spirit, and you will never fulfill the desires of the flesh.

17 For what the flesh wants is opposed to the Spirit, and what the Spirit wants is opposed to the flesh. They are opposed to each other, and so you don't do what you want to do.

18 But if you are being led by the Spirit, you are not under the Law.

19 Now the works of the flesh are obvious: sexual immorality, impurity, promiscuity,

20 idolatry, witchcraft, hatred, rivalry, jealously, outbursts of anger, quarrels, conflicts, factions,

21 envy, murder, drunkenness, wild partying, and things like that. I'm telling you now, as I've told you in the past, that people who practice such things will not inherit God's kingdom.

22 But the fruit of the Spirit is love, joy, peace, patience, kindness, goodness, faithfulness,

23 gentleness, and self-control. There is no law against such things.

24 Now those who belong to Christ Jesus have crucified their flesh with its passions and desires.

25 If we live by the Spirit, let us also be guided by the Spirit.

- Galatians 5:16-25 (ISV)

The above passage teaches that we can only live one of two kinds of life: either we live in the flesh or live in the Spirit. When we live in the flesh, our lives manifest different sins and evil. But when we live in the Spirit our lives reveal the character of Christ, called the Fruit of the Spirit here.

Making Real Changes

These passages I am about to detail here tell of real changes in the life of believers.

17 The story of what happened spread quickly all through Ephesus, to Jews and Greeks alike. A solemn fear descended on the city, and the name of the Lord Jesus was greatly honored.

18 Many who became believers confessed their sinful practices.

19 A number of them who had been practicing sorcery brought their incantation books and burned them at a public bonfire. The value of the books was several million dollars.

20 So the message about the Lord spread widely and had a powerful effect.

- Acts 19:17-20 (NLT2)

Here in Ephesus, a big city, we notice that new believers showed the power of Christ in their lives when they threw away all the books of magic and sorcery that they were consulting before. We must have our way of showing that real change has come into our lives, like Zacchaeus in the account below:

8 Meanwhile, Zacchaeus stood before the Lord and said, "I will give half my wealth to the poor, Lord, and if I have cheated people on their taxes, I will give them back four times as much!"

9 Jesus responded, "Salvation has come to this home today, for this man has shown himself to be a true son of Abraham.

10 For the Son of Man came to seek and save those who are lost."

- Luke 19:8-10 (NLT2)

When our Lord Jesus visited Zacchaeus, he took the opportunity to show repentance and change. More than that, he took the opportunity to make restitution for his sins.

You may check the following references yourself:

Romans 1:22-32; Romans 6:1-14; 1 Corinthians 5:1-13; 1 Corinthians 6:1-20;

Ephesians 4:17 – 32; Ephesians 5:1 – 21; Colossians 3:1 - 17

All these references speak about the new man or the new individual that should emerge after being born again. Some of them talk clearly about the sins of the old nature that we must get rid of, and the good we must begin to practice as children of God through Christ. When you look at the examples of change quoted above, that is, the brethren at Ephesus, and Zacchaeus, you will immediately notice an effort to live lives that reflect their conversion to Christ. The brethren at Ephesus had among them believers that still practiced magic or consulted mediums. There is still quite a lot of this today among church-going people who claim to believe in Jesus as Saviour. But once God's power touched these people, they made a clean break with such practices. In my experience, people have brought their charms and meditation books to be burnt or destroyed as proof of change. These are signs of genuine conversion.

Restitution

Notice that Zacchaeus went beyond repentance to show restitution. Restitution is the act of making reparation or paying back for things done in the past. Sometimes, the Spirit of the Lord will insist that we go through this as proof of our genuine conversion. Because some of these issues may prove embarrassing to admit, some people have tended to say that once a person has repented, there should be no need for restitution since the Lord has completely forgiven him or her.

There is no doubt that the Lord has fully forgiven, once an individual has genuinely repented. Sometimes, and I do mean occasionally, He may still want us to go ahead and make restitution. He will always urge it on us by stirring our spirit to it. And if the Lord is asking us to do this, then it is not helpful to ignore it as it will imply disobedience to the Lord's desire. I must hasten to add that restitution usually leads to inner healing of hurts in us and others, particularly when the Lord urges us to do it.

I once read of a man who used to drop his garbage in bits in front of his neighbours' doors early in the morning before they woke up. He always enjoyed watching them fume and rage. Then he got converted, and the Spirit of the Lord insisted that he go round and apologize. He was afraid of seeing the anger he had enjoyed causing at a distance now descend on him. But because he was convinced it was of the Lord, he asked Him for inner strength and so could do it.

That is a tough one, indeed. But why do you say sometimes and not always?

I do not think it is helpful to be legalistic about this since the Lord knows where it will help, and where it may hinder. That is why I prefer to ask the Holy Spirit to direct in this always. Sometimes, the Lord may say that restitution is required, but that the time is not yet. Untimely reparation may do more harm than good. If you do it when God urges it, it will always help one way or the other.

I think I understand what you mean.

One thing we must guard against though is hypocrisy as detailed below. This will lead to self-condemnation if we do not rigorously pursue a genuine change in our lives. We may even end up bringing shame to the name of Christ, as the passage here describes. The moment people know us as born-again Christians, then they would have certain expectations of us.

"You, therefore, who teach another, do you not teach yourself? You who preach that a man should not steal,

do you steal? You who say, do not commit adultery, do you commit adultery? You who abhor idols, do you rob temples? You who make your boast in the Law, do you dishonor God through breaking the Law? For the name of God is blasphemed among the Gentiles because of you, as it is written."

- Romans 2:17-24 [NKJV]

We do have a great responsibility to God and the body of believers to submit to the Holy Spirit of God to make these changes in us wherever we need them. There is something else you may need to bear in mind. The attitude of old friends

What is it?

Your friends may disapprove of your new-found life in Christ.

Don't I know that already?

Here is the way the Bible puts it:

1 Since Christ suffered physically, you must also strengthen yourselves with the same way of thinking that he had; because whoever suffers physically is no longer involved with sin.

2 From now on, then, you must live the rest of your earthly lives controlled by God's will and not by human desires.

3 You have spent enough time in the past doing what the heathen like to do. Your lives were spent in indecency, lust, drunkenness, orgies, drinking parties, and the disgusting worship of idols.

4 And now the heathen are surprised when you do not join them in the same wild and reckless living, and so they insult you.

5 But they will have to give an account of themselves to God, who is ready to judge the living and the dead.

- 1 Peter 4:1-5 (TEV)

HABITS

What about habits?

I am glad that you raised this question now because it will enable us to deal with a fundamental principle relating to an individual's walk before his God. Loyalty to God and His Christ demands that we make some value judgments in our lives. The Holy Spirit of God that lives within us will always guide us on this. I touched a little bit on this earlier when I was talking about restitution.

When God promised to make a new covenant with man, part of that promise envisaged that every child of God should tap from the resources of the Word of God – the Bible, and the communion of the indwelling Holy Spirit to straighten out their life before God. Here is the way the prophet Jeremiah put it:

³³ *"Instead, this is the covenant I will make with the house of Israel after those days"* — *the LORD's declaration. "I will put my teaching within them and write it on their hearts. I will be their God, and they will be my people.*

³⁴ *No longer will one teach his neighbor or his brother, saying, 'Know the Lord,' for they will all know me, from the least to the greatest of them"* — *this is the LORD's declaration. "For I will forgive their iniquity and never again remember their sin.*

- Jeremiah 31:33-34 (CSB Bible)

The new covenant of grace in Christ Jesus provides for the Holy Spirit's daily guidance in the life of the individual, particularly in areas like habits. In Romans 8:14, the Bible states that as many as are led by the Spirit of God, are the sons of God. We shall look at this in closer detail later.

But there is a Bible passage that adequately provides a guiding principle. Here is what it says:

"All things are lawful unto me, but all things are not expedient: all things are lawful for me, but I will not be brought under the power of any."

- 1st Corinthians 6:12 [NKJV]

Here is the rendering in a more modern translation:

1 Corinthians 6:12 (TLB)

[12] *I can do anything I want to if Christ has not said no, but some of these things aren't good for me. Even if I am allowed to do them, I'll refuse to if I think they might get such a grip on me that I can't easily stop when I want to.*

The whole point about habits is that many of them affect us in a way that our resolve or will is weakened. This damage may prove so severe that it enslaves us, making us do so many things we would not have done otherwise. Take alcohol, for instance, it has a disinhibiting effect; that is, it loosens people up and lowers their moral and spiritual resolve. The same goes for any and every habit-forming drug. They create a kind of dependence that is false, and they undoubtedly do becloud thinking and judgment at high blood levels. King Solomon, who drank quite a bit indeed, had these to say:

"It is not for kings O Lemuel - not for kings to drink wine, Nor for princes intoxicating drink; Lest they drink and forget the Law, and pervert the justice of all the afflicted. Give strong drink to him who is perishing and wine to those who are bitter of heart." [Proverbs 31:4-6 NIV]

"Wine is a mocker, intoxicating drink arouses brawling, And whoever is led astray by it is not wise." [Proverbs 20:1 NIV]

"Who has woe? Who has sorrow? Who has strife? Who has complaints? Who has needless bruises? Who has bloodshot eyes? Those who linger over wine, who go to sample bowls of mixed wine. Do not gaze at wine when it is red, when it sparkles in the cup when it goes down

smoothly! In the end, it bites like a snake and poisons like a viper. Your eyes will see strange sights, and your mind imagine confusing things." [Proverbs 23:29-33 NIV]

Some argue that Paul admonished Timothy not to take water only but to use a little wine for his stomach's sake. As a physician by profession, I think I can identify with that in the sense that it may have been some commonplace prescription for such indigestion, just like someone would recommend antacids today. Some describe themselves as social drinkers who feel that they do not have a habit to talk about since they do not indulge. There is a passage that the Lord has used to keep many believers safely away from the bottle. Here is what it says:

"And be not drunk with wine wherein is excess; but be filled with the Spirit."

- Ephesians 5:18 [KJV]

Whereas they recognize that what is in question here is excess drinking, they also have not failed to notice that alcohol and spirituality seem to be at opposite poles. In other words, the less you have of alcohol, the easier it is for you to discern the Holy Spirit and His moves in your life. It is interesting to note that the Nazarites in the Old Testament, close to God by calling, were not allowed to touch any alcohol by Law. You may notice that I have discussed this question rather openly. This is as it should be. You may take time to search the Scriptures in more detail on this question of habits and ask the Holy Spirit to help you make up your mind.

However, if you know that you already do have a serious problem with any of these habits, such an exercise would only serve to continue to have you enslaved by it. The best thing is to ask the LORD to give you the power to break loose in Jesus's mighty name.

It is also important to note that the whole thing has ceased to be a simple habit for some people. A spiritual force is now using alcohol or the like drug to destroy their lives. If that is your experience, then you will need to be delivered from that bondage. You can see that given all these potentials for evil, most Christians prefer to stay well away from the bottle, and the like habit-forming drugs.

But some habits are not mentioned in the Bible.

You are quite correct there. However, the Bible has general principles to guide a Christian who is sincerely in doubt, to determine what the mind of God is in every situation. It is always good to remember that the Christian perspective to life, in general, is often not well appreciated until one is born again. The Bible said as much in 1st Corinthians 2:14-16.

"But the man who isn't a Christian can't understand and can't accept these thoughts from God, which the Holy Spirit teaches us. They sound foolish to him because only those who have the Holy Spirit within them can understand what the Holy Spirit means. Others just can't take it in. But the spiritual man has insight into everything, and that bothers and baffles the man of the world, who can't understand him at all. How could he? For certainly, he has never been one to know the Lord's thoughts, or to discuss them with him, or to move the hands of God by prayer. But, strange as it seems, we Christians actually do have within us a portion of the very thoughts and mind of Christ." [LB]

I am sure you can appreciate the above passage. I certainly can. Before I became born again myself, I thought a lot of these things were just funny. Now I know better. But let us look at some of these principles in God's word, which help us make up our minds on these habits.

The Temple of the Holy Spirit

Your body is the temple of the Holy Spirit of God, and so must be kept pure for the Lord. The Bible puts it this way:

"Do you not know that you are the temple of God and that the Spirit of God dwells in you? If anyone defiles the temple of God, God will destroy him. For the temple of God is holy, which temple you are. Let no one deceive himself. If anyone of you seems to be wise in this age, let him become a fool that he may become wise. For the wisdom of this world is foolishness with God. For it is written, He catches the wise in their craftiness, and again, The Lord knows the thoughts of the wise that they are futile."

- 1st Corinthians 3:16-20 [NKJV]

God's Desire for Our Health

God's desire for us is to be in health and not to take those things we know are injurious to our health. The Bible puts it this way.

"Beloved, I pray that you may prosper in all things and be in health, just as your soul prospers." [3rd John vs. 2 NKJ]

Strength in the Inner Man

It is the will of God that we have strength in the inner man. This is the strength we need to resolve all these conflicts to empower us to make spiritual progress heavenward. This inner resolve is so essential for doing the will of God that we should welcome every opportunity to develop it. The Bible puts it this way.

"For this reason I bow my knees to the Father of our Lord Jesus Christ from whom the whole family in heaven and earth is named that He would grant you according to the riches of His glory, to be strengthened with might through his spirit in the inner man." [Ephesians 3:14-16 NKJV]

One may go on and lay many more principles, but I suppose that these are enough. They are sufficient to guide us through several indulgences, whether with food or drinks, or stimulant bearing drugs like tobacco or cigarettes and other such issues.

Here is something I find very useful, which you may find helpful: it is to be downright honest before the Lord. I know that there is one other thing that deters spiritual progress, and that is arguing with the voice of the Spirit of God in your life. If God says quit, there is no need looking for somebody to tell you that it does not matter that much. The issue is not that fundamental. Indeed it may not be, but the Spirit of the Lord within you has said to you: 'QUIT!' You had better. The gain will always be yours.

DAILY BIBLE STUDY

I would like to have a good knowledge of the Bible too.

You certainly can. It is not unusual for one to wonder whether he can ever have such a working grasp of God's word. I felt the same way soon after I gave my life to Christ. A Professor of pathology, a very brilliant one for that matter once said to me: I can't quote the Bible the way you do. I simply told him that it was a matter of time and diligent study. There is one thing that helps an individual develop an aggressively healthy Bible study habit. It is the Berean Christians' approach to Christian growth:

"And the brethren immediately sent away Paul and Silas by night unto Be-re-a: who coming thither went into the synagogue of the Jews. These were more noble than those in Thess-a-lo-ni-ca, in that they received the word with all readiness of mind, and searched the

scriptures daily, whether those things were so." [Acts 17:10,11 KJV]

A person who has just been born again and is regularly attending a fellowship or church is hearing a lot and learning a lot rather rapidly. He needs to take time daily to check the Scriptures so that his learning will consolidate in his thoughts.

Quiet Time

One way to do this is to develop a habit generally referred to as QUIET TIME. This is a time one has set aside to study the Bible and to pray every day. It is often better early in the morning before one starts the day. Initially, one may set aside half-an-hour to study and meditate on God's word and pray. A Bible reading guide is usually quite useful at this stage. Although it breaks up the passages into small portions, it assists the individual to learn a little truth at a time. Later on, one may need to get Bible study Bibles with cross-references, as well as a study Concordance that will help locate Bible verses. There are also more detailed Bible study courses that are quite useful. Any Christian bookshop will help with details.

These days there is a variety of computer software that can mimic going to a Bible College. Through the software, one can acquire a Christian library of over a thousand books that will include commentaries, encyclopedias, various translations of the Bible with their cross-references, and books, including biographies and systematic theology, Bible history, Church history and more. Technology has greatly enhanced our capacity to study the Bible and learn in our own time, and the internet will furnish you with several options from which to choose. Also, I have found audio Bible CDs very useful for gaining a rapid overview of the Bible. An overview creates familiarity with several passages of the Bible, making in-depth study much more accessible. The software then comes in handy when trying to find quotes you know about but cannot locate the Book of the Bible, the chapter or the verse from where they come.

Are there some other tips that may be useful?

Indeed there are. For example, it took me quite some time to realize that the Bible is a revelation of God to man. And that beginning from Genesis, all the way to the book of Revelation, the task before the individual is to discover God, His ways, His likes and dislikes, and how He has made it possible for us as individuals to get to know Him personally. In the process, we learn a lot about ourselves, how God sees us, and how God expects us to see ourselves and our fellow men.

After I came to this realization, it gave my Bible study a practical orientation. The stories that I read, whether in the Old or New Testaments, reveal something about God. So I must not take them in isolation. I must look for what they tell about God. This sort of background is panoramic and helps to put things in their proper perspective. You may find it useful.

Daily Prayers

Now that you have mentioned quiet time, I might as well tell you that I do not know how to pray. I have heard quite many people say that. From all my discussions with them, I have come to realize what the problem truly is. Many of these people have come to believe that effective prayer is said in a certain way: far from it. Remember that when one is born again, he has entered into a father-son or daughter relationship with God.

When children talk to their parents, they are supposed to speak respectfully. They usually should feel free to speak out their minds, especially where a good, warm, and affectionate family relationship exists.

When people go to God and repeatedly try to say some special words in a particular way they have learned, they create the impression that they are under the stranglehold of religion. The reason is that what they are saying may bear no relationship to the pressures they are facing, which is weighing heavily on their minds. Let us take a simple example.

A factory is having a downturn in its finances. Management has decided that the best way to solve the problem is to prune the staff's strength down by retrenching some workers. Nobody knows who and who will be affected. There is so much uncertainty. If only new orders would come in, the management may reconsider the retrenchment option.

A Christian member of staff is among those facing the retrenchment option. He goes home to his family with this news, and together they search out an 'appropriate prayer' and begin to recite it until they are weary, and all fall asleep. That is what I choose to call the religious approach, and this appropriate prayer may be repeated every day for as long as the situation persists. God is usually not expected to say anything. You will need a particular prophet or diviner to get His input from Him.

As a result of this, many run off in search of diviners and astrologers to assist with predicting the future. The Bible has something to say about that:

"There shall not be found among you anyone who makes his son or his daughter pass through the fire, or one who practices witchcraft, or a soothsayer, or one who interprets omens, or a sorcerer, or one who conjures spells, or a medium, or a spiritualist or one

who calls up the dead. For all who do these things are an abomination to the Lord..." [Deuteronomy 18:10 - 12NKJV]

A Christian who has learned to converse with God, may find a quiet corner somewhere and discuss the relevant issues as one should do in a conversation between a father and his son or daughter.

"Dear Lord, what do you think about the problem we have in the office? I am in danger of retrenchment in these challenging times. Please, Lord, You have to come to our aid. The situation is bad enough as it is, and this may prove the very last straw for many of us unless You intervene. Dear Lord, are there spiritual forces at work in our factory that may be responsible for this turn of events, or is this a simple case of poor judgment and poor management? Please speak to me, Lord, I need to know what is going on. Naturally, You can see I am concerned, but I want to tell You that I am confident that You will take care of me no matter what happens.

I have committed my life and future into Your hands, and I am quite content to leave them there."

This type of dialogue prayer will sooner than later, elicit a response from the Lord which the individual can appreciate, as the Spirit of the Lord ministers to his heart. The Spirit of God will convey the mind of God about the situation to the individual. Once a person can hear God on a particular issue, then whatever the Lord says, is what will be. This is because whatever the Lord says is truth par excellence- that is, the situation as it actually is or is soon to be.

You make it sound very simple. I am sure it is not that simple.

I think the simplest way to put it is that *anybody who can talk can pray*. I once read about a man who went to God to complain about some members of his church. He wanted the Lord to change them and make them more like Christ or words to that effect. The Lord told him he was the one who needed the change. His only problem was that they did not allow him to dominate them or something like that. But this is the sort of x-ray that goes on before the Lord.

Take the above example of the factory worker, for instance; God may point out to the Christian how their union actions have contributed to the situation, and how he had failed in the past to speak up about excesses of the union leaders. The most satisfying thing about going to God with a situation is that you will soon get to find out the correct position of things and if any remedy is available.

I wish it were as easy as you make it sound.

Initial difficulties exist with getting to know whether it is the Lord who is speaking. But the only way to overcome such a problem is by asking Him repeatedly to talk to you.

You can bet I will begin to try this out today.

That would be wonderful, indeed. The result will amaze you. What you will discover is that the more you make an effort to wait to hear from the Lord, the easier and faster the communication channel becomes, and the richer your testimony of God's reality in your life.

3.

DOCTRINES

I am worried about doctrine.

Putting together a set of cardinal beliefs is not as simple as it sounds. The Bible reveals principles and patterns of following the invisible God. Therefore one has to be sure that whatever he/she believes about God or about life and the way to live, it must have support in the Bible. I had to take this position to protect myself from all manners of doctrines.

After I made this decision, I began to examine my beliefs in the light of God's Word. I discovered many new things that I did not know before. I also found a lot of my religious practices that were indefensible from Scripture.

Afterward, I was able to determine those that had no spiritual significance that had to be done away with and those I could deemphasize for lack of merit. I suppose this will depend on your pre-born-again background. But every practice should be judged by Scripture. Our Lord Jesus commanded us to search the Scriptures in John chapter 5 and verse 39.

I believe this is a very safe approach, mainly because going to God's heaven where Jesus is, is a solemn business. You may need further help in this area, and you should consult your base counselors for more clarification.

There are, however, some doctrines that the Bible describes as fundamental or foundational. You may find some in Hebrews chapter six, verses one to three.

"Therefore leaving the discussion of the elementary principles of Christ, let us go on to perfection, not laying again the foundation of repentance from dead works and of faith toward God, of the doctrine of baptisms, of laying on of hands, of resurrection of the dead, and of eternal judgment." [Hebrews.6:1-3 NKJ]

Let us look at some of these briefly.

Repentance from Dead Works

The best way to appreciate this is to look at a few passages that speak directly about it. But before we do that, it may be necessary to point out that what is in question here is not works for work's sake but works as a basis for acceptance before the Almighty God. The Bible describes it as dead works because they are incapable of making an individual right before God.

The works here referred to includes keeping of the laws, which will include the Ten Commandments. The whole point here is that nobody has ever, nor can anybody ever keep all the Law. So, since one cannot observe all the Law all the time, it is more profitable to come to God by grace through faith always to be forgiven and accepted because of the sacrifice of our Lord and Saviour Jesus Christ.

"Now we know that whatever the Law says, it says to those who are under the Law so that every mouth may be silenced and the whole world held accountable to God. Therefore no-one will be declared righteous in his sight by observing the Law; rather through the Law we become conscious of sin. But now righteousness from God, apart from Law, has been made known, to which the Law and the Prophets testify. This righteousness from God comes through faith in Jesus Christ to all who believe. There is no difference, for all have sinned and fall short of the glory of God and are justified freely by his grace through the redemption that came by Christ Jesus."

-Romans. 3:19-24 [NIV]

Here is the way Apostle James described the weakness in the Law as a means of salvation:

10For the person who keeps all of the laws except one is as guilty as a person who has broken all of God's laws. James 2:10 [NLT2]

You may wonder if this means that Christians do not obey the Ten Commandments. No, it doesn't mean that. What it does mean is that by following the Holy Spirit, a Christian obeys more than the demands of the Ten Commandments. This is what Jesus implied in Matthew 5:20 where He said:

"For I tell you that unless your righteousness surpasses that of the Pharisees and the teachers of the law, you will certainly not enter the Kingdom of God." [NIV]

For example, one of the laws in the Ten Commandments has to do with adultery. Let us look at what Jesus had to say on this:

"You have heard that it was said. Do not commit adultery. But I tell you that anyone who looks at a woman lustfully has already committed adultery with her in his heart."

- Matthew 5:.27,28 [NIV]

This is the point expressly made by the apostle Paul in his letter to the Romans where he said:

"There is therefore now no condemnation to those who are in Christ Jesus, who do not work according to the flesh, but according to the Spirit. For the Law of the Spirit of life in Christ Jesus has made me free from the Law of sin and death. For what the Law could not do in that it was weak through the flesh, God did by sending His own Son in the likeness of sinful flesh, on account of sin: He condemned sin in the flesh, that the righteous requirement of the Law might be fulfilled in us who do not work according to the flesh but according to the Spirit."

- Romans 8:1-4 [NKJV]

So, the demands of the Law, including the Ten Commandments, are more than met in those who follow the Spirit of God's leading. And when a person is born again, he is supposed to learn to follow the Spirit of God progressively.

Therefore, repentance from dead works means that we are not trusting in anything we can do to justify us before God. But conscious of the fact that *'all our righteousness are like filthy rags before God'* [Isaiah 64:6], we should continuously plead the grace of God and the blood of redemption or reconciliation that was shed for us by Jesus Christ when we appear before God.

Faith Toward God

Hebrews 11:6, gives us a good picture of what is here implied:

"But without faith, it is impossible to please Him, for he who comes to God must believe that He is and that He is a rewarder of those who diligently seek Him." *[NKJ]*

The Bible reminds us that;

"No one has seen God at any time..."

- John 1:18 [NKJ].

Again it tells us that this is because:

"God is a Spirit, and they that worship Him must worship Him in Spirit and in truth."

- John 4:24 [KJV].

Therefore, it follows that since no one has seen God, the only way to relate and sense God is through the quickened human spirit and so by faith. This is because faith is the only sensor of the spirit. The physical has five senses of touch, sight, hearing, taste, and smell. But the spirit has only one sensor, FAITH. Faith will enable the individual to experience the reality of God in his life and circumstances. Faith is what helps a man to know God. It is faith that produces the experience; experience delivers the assurance of the reality of God and His interventionist roles in the life and circumstances of the believer. Faith invariably leads to the supernatural or miraculous, which may be so designated either because of its nature or its timing. The relationship between belief in God and experience is why the Bible declares without equivocation that;

"The just shall live by faith." [Romans 1:17]

Again it says;

10 So those who believe in the Son of God have this testimony in their own heart, but those who do not believe God, have made a liar of Him because they have not believed what God has said about His Son.

11The testimony is this: God has given us eternal life, and this life has its source in His Son.

12Whoever has the Son has this life; whoever does not have the Son of God does not have life.

- James 2:10 [NLT2]

I will mention one more of the foundational doctrines in some detail but will summarize the rest. One gets to learn a lot more with time. Let us talk about the *Doctrine of Baptisms*.

The Doctrine of Baptisms

The fact that baptisms rather than baptism was used here suggests that there must be at least more than one, and indeed there are two cardinal ones, namely: Water Baptism and Holy Ghost Baptism.

Water Baptism

This follows the experience of the new birth. Where most people usually have some problem is if they were baptized as infants. Some argue that God should be able to transfer their infant baptism to count for their post-conversion fulfillment of all righteousness as our Lord Jesus called it.

Baptism is symbolic of repentance. The very word means to immerse. So when a person is immersed in water, it signifies his death to sin; when he emerges from the water, it indicates his match to a new life. As the perfect man, our Lord Jesus did not need baptism, but yet He submitted to it.

"Then Jesus came from Galilee to John at the Jordan to be baptized by him. And John tried to prevent Him, saying, I have need to be baptized by You, and are You coming to me? But Jesus answered and said to him. Permit it to be so now, for thus it is fitting for us to fulfill all righteousness. Then he allowed Him."
- *Matthew 3:13-15 [NKJ]*

When Peter preached his great sermon on the day of Pentecost, he urged the people to repent, and be baptized. The implication is that baptism is for those who had repented. [Acts 2:38]

Someone may say, 'But this is why we ask them to come for confirmation so that they can re-affirm the faith made on their behalf by their god-parents.' Indeed it may be so for some of the people. But I would prefer to fulfill all righteousness like our Lord Himself did, rather than stick to tradition. I have always taken the injunction or warning of the apostle Paul in Colossians 2:8 to heart.

"Beware lest anyone cheat you through philosophy and empty deceit, according to the tradition of men, according to the basic principles of the world, and not according to Christ." [NKJV]

It might be necessary to find somewhere where a group is organizing the believer's baptism and be baptized there if your group does not organize it. I went through a believer's baptism at a convention that was inter-denominational. I went ahead and fulfilled all righteousness, just like our Lord Jesus did.

Holy Ghost Baptism

Since the Bible is the final authority for all doctrine and conduct for the Christian, the best thing is to look at what it has to say. Our Lord Jesus Christ commissioned the disciples to go into the entire world and preach the gospel. But they needed Holy Ghost power.

"Then He opened their minds to understand at last these many Scriptures! And He said, Yes, it was written long ago that the Messiah must suffer and die and rise again from the dead on the third day; and that this message of salvation should be taken from Jerusalem to all the nations: There is forgiveness of sins for all who turn to me. You have seen these prophecies come true.

And now I will send the Holy Spirit upon you, just as my Father promised. Don't begin telling others yet - stay here in the city until the Holy Spirit comes and fills you with power from heaven."

- Luke 24:45-49 [LB]

Our Lord Jesus felt His disciples needed the Holy
Ghost baptism to face the challenges of Christian
witness. We have another record of it.

*"During the forty days after his crucifixion, he
appeared to the apostles from time to time, actually
alive, and proved to them in many ways that it was
really he himself they were seeing. And on these
occasions, he talked to them about the kingdom of God.
In one of these meetings, he told them not to leave
Jerusalem until the Holy Spirit came upon them in
fulfillment of the Father's promise, a matter he had
previously discussed with them."*

- Acts 1:3-4 [TLB]

*"But when the Holy Spirit has come upon you, you will
receive power to testify of me with great effect, to the
people in Jerusalem, throughout Judea, in Samaria, and
to the ends of the earth, about my death and
resurrection."*

- Actsl:8 [TLB]

We can conclude from these passages that the apostles needed the Holy Ghost baptism to witness about Christ. The question then is, do we in this generation need the same experience? Should we, too, expect to receive the same experience? Let us see what the apostle Peter said to the crowd on Pentecost's day, the day he received his own Holy Ghost baptism.

"And Peter replied, Each one of you must turn from sin, return to God, and be baptized in the name of Jesus Christ for the forgiveness of your sins; then you also shall receive this gift, the Holy Spirit. For Christ promised him to each one of you who has been called by the Lord our God, and to your children and even to those in distant lands."

- Acts 2:38,39 [TLB]

Some people say that the Holy Ghost baptism was only necessary for the early apostles. The fact is that there is nothing we can find in Scripture to justify such a conclusion. Instead, what we see is a concerted effort by the early apostles to ensure that anyone who believed in Christ in their time, also received the Holy Ghost Baptism.

"When the apostles back in Jerusalem heard that the people of Samaria had accepted God's message, they sent down Peter and John. As soon as they arrived, they began praying for these new Christians to receive the Holy Spirit, for as yet He has not come upon any of them: For they had only been baptized in the name of the Lord Jesus.

Then Peter and John laid their hands upon these believers, and they received the Holy Spirit."

- Acts 8:14-17 [TLB]

From Paul's encounter with certain disciples in Ephesus in Acts 19, verses 1 to 7, we can discern the same trend. He had pointedly asked them: "Did you receive the Holy Spirit when you believed?" The implication being that there were people here and there then, who may have believed, but had not received.

Just like there were people in those days that had believed in Christ but had not received the Holy Spirit, so also today, we have people who have believed but have not received. There are many people here and there who have accepted Christ but have not received the Holy Spirit.

Therefore, it behooves all of us who minister, to seek out those who are yet to receive the baptism of the Holy Spirit, and as the early apostles did, help them receive the Holy Spirit baptism as the apostles received at the very beginning, complete with the accompanying signs of tongues and prophecy.[Acts 10:44-46, and 11:15-17]

I would prefer that we leave off the rest of the foundational doctrines until later. There is always time to catch up on Laying on of Hands, the Resurrection of the Dead, and Eternal Judgement.

4.

OTHER CONCERNS

I have other concerns

I would like to know what these fresh concerns are, so we can talk about them too before we end.

I really do thank God very much that He came down and saved me. But I am worried about whether I will be able to stay a born-again Christian for a long time. You know, whatever you may say, I know that Christian life is a big challenge in a corrupt society and with several inherent corrupting influences.

There is no doubt about the genuineness of your concerns. Incidentally, I had those concerns myself a few months after I was born again. But certain things will help any of us stay on course without consciously making a special effort. I learned about some of these after a while, and I would share them with you now.

Witnessing

Witnessing involves getting others to come and know the Lord Jesus Christ as their personal Lord and Saviour, just like you have done. You may wonder: so soon! Yes, indeed, the sooner, the better. Look at the way the Bible puts it:

"For if you tell others with your own mouth that Jesus Christ is your Lord, and believe in your own heart that God has raised Him from the dead, you will be saved. For it is by believing in his heart that a man becomes right with God, and with his mouth, he tells others of

his faith, confirming his salvation." [Romans. 10:9,10 LB]

Just like this Scripture has said, there is nothing that strengthens your faith as much as sharing it with others. After I gave my life to Christ, I told my family's immediate members, my brothers, and sisters. Then I sat down and wrote to all my friends that I had now become a born-again Christian. It does strengthen your faith a great deal I can tell you. Besides, there is one other thing it does for you?

What is it?

It puts a kind of check on you immediately if people know that you are now born again. You know, some people may not like that at all.

Yes!

But anyone serious about his or her faith will welcome that. It's like serving notice at home or work that you are now ready to ply the straight and narrow way. People are bound to keep an eye on you and say: "Hey, I thought you were born again? How come you are still into this kind of stuff?" It helps you face the responsibility you now owe to Christ and His body here on earth to straighten up and order your life in conformity with God's Word. You may not like it initially, but I can tell you, it does help to have people around who can say that to you.

Huh!

I recall an experience of years ago. As an undergraduate medical student, we were just returning from an anatomy dissection class, and a Christian friend of mine was trying to witness. Then my friends and classmates said something about me that shocked me:

What did they say?

Here's what they said: "We like Okey's type of Christianity," [meaning me]; "He does not disturb anybody." You can see that it was indeed a grave indictment. After that, I went home and cried to God to make my faith disturb this "sleep of death" in the lives of my friends and colleagues. Besides this, there is another significant reason why we should witness or tell others about our Lord Jesus Christ. In fact, it is a more important reason.

I would like to hear that too.

Our Lord and Saviour Jesus Christ commanded us to witness, and He expects us to obey. The way He put it in the Bible, there isn't much choice for His follower, someone who has accepted Him as his or her Lord and Saviour.

"And then he told them, [meaning the believers], You are to go into all the world and preach the Good News to everyone, everywhere. Those who believe and are

baptized will be saved. But those who refuse to believe will be condemned." [Mark. 16:15,16 TLB]

This particular command helps me answer some of my friends and colleagues who claim they were born again, too, like me, but that the only difference between us is that they did not carry their Bibles about and disturb people the way I did. "Christianity," they say, "is a personal thing. You should just keep it to yourself."

I think so too!

But as you can see now, there is no way a born-again Christian can hide the Light of God shining in him or her. Our Lord Jesus expects us to put that light on the table so that others can see it and walk by it.

This you may check out for yourself in Matthew chapter 5, verses 13 to 16.

Reservations about witnessing

I can see I will have a problem with witnessing: Not just a problem but also lots of issues.

What sort of problems are these?

The first one is that I am a timid person. I hardly talk to people about myself. I wonder how I can cope with this. Besides, what will I be saying to them? I hardly know what the whole thing is about myself? You know, people generally argue a lot about these things. I will just be making a fool of myself. And I can tell you for sure, nobody will believe me out there. You know, preachers look somehow; forceful, convincing, and charismatic: I am not just that way, and I just don't like rejection.

And what I can't stand is the sneer from all those guys: "even you too." No. It will almost kill me. I used to pity those guys who came around talking about their faith. The guys used to give

them real hard time, and you can bet I did join them some of the time.

That is a whole lot of reservations. One thing I will like to tell you is that if you go out of that door and count one hundred Christians who are witnessing, one hundred of them will tell you that they had some reservations initially, beginning with yours sincerely.

Your very first reservation, shyness, was my first reservation too. I enjoyed my faith, but I had difficulties talking about it. I was to discover later, that what I needed was the anointing and quickening of the Holy Spirit.

You will need to explain a little more about that.

There is one man in the Bible whose experience is quite helpful. You remember that when our Lord Jesus was about to be crucified, Peter denied three times that he had ever met Him. He couldn't stand up to a young lady to say: "Yes, I know the man;

in fact, He is my Lord and Master." [Mark 14:66-72]. But on the day of Pentecost and subsequent occasions, he was the chief spokesman of the early disciples. [Acts chapters 1,2,3 and 4]. Let me reproduce a prayer; you may find it helpful. The early apostles themselves said it.

"And now, O Lord, hear their threats, and grant to thy servants great boldness in their preaching, and send your healing power, and may miracles and wonders be done by the name of thy holy servant Jesus."
- *Acts 4:29,30 [LB]*

This is how the Lord answered this prayer for them.

"After this prayer, the building where they were meeting shook, and they were all filled with the Holy Spirit and boldly preached God's message."
- *Acts 4:31 [LB]*

From all these, you can see that one can begin to ask the Lord for the Spirit of boldness to preach

God's Word. Soon you will discover, just like I did, that the whole shyness is gone and that God has a treasure in you that has been lying idle all these years.

I really do hope and pray so.

Now, let us look at your second reservation; lack of knowledge of God's word. This may look like such a significant handicap initially, but it helps to remember that we are called to be witnesses of what we have seen, heard, or experienced. [1st John 1:1-4] If you have ever been to a court, you would have noticed that witnesses are asked to speak about what they saw or heard. If they are honest witnesses, they would not have any difficulties with that, and their story will be consistent each time.

In John 9:1-34, the blind man that our Lord Jesus healed demonstrated the powers of a genuine experience of an encounter with Jesus.

You need to get your Bible and read it. Let me summarize the story.

This gentleman was born blind. Our Lord Jesus, came by him and healed him. When the Jewish leaders heard about it, they called him and asked him about it. In fact, some people wondered if he was indeed the same person. He left them in no doubt. He owned up.

When asked how he came to be seeing, he told a simple story. Jesus made a paste of sand, rubbed it on my eyes, and asked me to wash it out, and when I did, I came back seeing. These are simple facts of his experience. The leaders did not believe him, so they called his parents to ascertain whether he was indeed the same blind beggar they all knew. His parents confirmed that he was, but they could not tell how he came now to be seeing. Then the leaders asked what appears to be a theological question about Jesus being a sinner. The man replied with common sense logic, supplied by the Holy Spirit.

"I don't know whether he is good or bad, the man replied, but I know this: I was blind, and now I see!" John 9:25 [LB]

This story is often the crux of the message of a witness.

- "I know what I used to be before I met Jesus Christ."

- "I know where, when, and how I met Him."

- "I know what has happened to me since I met Him."

- "You can come and share this experience with me."

Anybody who has had a genuine conversion experience can always share this kind of testimony. There is not much of theology there. But where someone raises theological questions beyond you, you may resort to what I choose to call invitational witnessing. Here is an example.

"The next day Jesus decided to go to Galilee. He found Philip and told him, Come with me. [You may say that Philip is now converted] Philip now went off to look for Nathanael and told him, We have found the Messiah! - the very person Moses and the prophets told about! His name is Jesus, the son of Joseph from Nazareth!

Nazareth! Exclaimed Nathanael. Can anything good come from there? [You may call this a *theological question] Just come and see for yourself, Philip declared."* - John 1:43, 45, 46 [LB]

Indeed one may not be able to answer all the vital questions an honest enquirer may ask. But you may lead them to Church, Fellowship, or Bible Class where they can get more help. With time, however, you will be able to pick-up fundamental concepts of the faith to confront a potential convert to our Lord Jesus Christ. I have found the Ten Commandments (Exodus 20:1-17) useful in recent times. I use them to create a consciousness of sin and an awareness of the consequences of continuing sinfulness.(Ezekiel 18:4; Romans 3:20,23 and 6:23, Galatians 3:24) I believe this is particularly useful in a society that has become very permissive, and where value systems have become quite relative.(Proverbs 28:13,16:25, 29:1) The Holy Ghost often uses this approach to bring about conviction in the heart of the hearer. (Acts 2:37-39)

A person under conviction is ready to hear about the grace and the mercy of God in Christ Jesus (Romans 5:7,8; Ephesians 1:7), which he or she subsequently comes to embrace with joy and gratitude. (Ephesians 2:8 and 9; Isaiah 1:18-20)

Your third reservation is that of rejection. One thing that is helpful in this regard is to bear in mind that a witness does not convert anybody. He simply tells his or her story as honestly and as convincingly as he or she can. The rest of the work of conviction and conversion of the hearers belongs to the Holy Spirit. It is always good to bear this in mind. If the hearer is willing to make a commitment of his or her life to the Lord, then you should seize the opportunity and lead them in the prayer of repentance and surrender of their lives to Christ.

One must never judge the effectiveness of his or her witnessing activities by the immediate result or statistics. God keeps the records in eternity. Indeed, you may never know that what you said so casually found fertile soil in your listener's heart. But eternity will reveal it. A person who surrenders his life to Christ today may be a by-product of the effort of several witnesses. The earlier witnesses served to water the soil of their heart for the seed to grow in due season, at the fullness of time. If you open your Bible to 1st Corinthians chapter 3, from verse 5, you will make this same discovery.

"My work was to plant the seed in your hearts, and Apollos' work was to water it, but it was God, not we, who made the garden grow in your hearts.

The person who does the planting or watering isn't very important, but God is important because he is the one who makes things grow.

Apollos and I are working as a team, with the same aim, though each one of us will be rewarded for his own hard work.

We are only God's co-workers." [1st Corinthians 3:6-9 TLB]

That is quite revealing indeed, and positively quite helpful to know.

In the light of this, it is impossible to say categorically that your witness was not well received since you cannot see into their hearts. It is often quite helpful not to make too much of what people are saying or how they react. Your experience may be able to tell you that a lot of that is a mere facade, or bravado, used to hide a deep need. And often behind all that, the Holy Spirit of God has found some fertile soil to bury your precious seed.

I pray so.

A lot of what I have said above goes for the sneers from your peers. Sometimes behind all that ridicule, lies a solemn wish to obtain what you have. But out of pride and peer pressure, they join others to ridicule something they sincerely desire. Those who have the courage of their convictions will always dare to be different from the crowd.

I certainly do agree with that.

And if you did dare to be different to become born again, then you must believe that your friends one day will do so too. I am amazed by the number of my school mates who used to sneer and laugh in those days, who now meet me in conventions and say: "Guess what? I, too, am born again." All I do is jump and shout, Praise the Lord! Only eternity will reveal whether I was one of those who started them on the road to faith in our Lord Jesus Christ.

I hope you have been able to see that you can begin right away to share your faith with others. If you ask the Lord in prayer to bless every word you speak and let it find fertile soil in the hearts of your hearers, the results will amaze you. Again if you ask the Lord in prayer to give you the right words, the result will equally be surprising. Matthew 10:19, speaks of being given the right words at the right time by the Holy Spirit of God.

Role Model

But permit me to share yet another reservation: One too many if you insist.

You do not need to worry about that. You will soon discover that virtually all of us had all kinds of reservations initially. That you feel entirely free to talk about them, I consider an excellent sign that you are willing to adequately address your issue.

I feel encouraged by that. I was beginning to wonder.

You don't need to.

O.K. then! I wonder whether I will not end up becoming like one of the Christians that I know. He is so quiet, so soft-spoken and so ascetic. The picture he paints scares me. I cannot even recommend that to myself, not to talk of re-fashioning another person into that kind of mould.

What you will discover when you study the lives of the followers of our dear Lord and Saviour Jesus Christ in the Bible, very closely, is that they were different personalities. There were extroverts like Peter, emotional, effusive, and sometimes explosive; there were introverts like John, deep, meditative, and more. There were also skeptics like Thomas, who needed facts to be convinced. The significant thing at the end of the day is that God Almighty transformed each person and used their natural attributes to extend and expand the Kingdom of God on earth in others.

A person like Apostle Paul, you may describe as a 'bulldozer,' an action man. "If you believe it, then go ahead and do it; don't hang around and talk about it." If you look at the Book of Acts, you will discover that he was like that before converting to Christ. He initially believed that the Christians were wrong, so he made every effort to eliminate them. When he got convinced that they were right, after all, he reversed gear with the same zeal and energy and planted the gospel of our Lord Jesus Christ in many parts of Europe and Palestine. Besides, he was very intellectual. From the Bible, you could see how God used that to provide us with a lot that is useful today.

We may conclude this by saying that God does not want you to be like someone else. He just wants to transform you and use you, whether you are noisy or quiet, extroverted or introverted, ascetic, or otherwise. The Bible urges us in Hebrews 12:2, to keep our eyes on Jesus. If we find something worth emulating in another brother or sister, the Holy Spirit may use that excellent way to encourage something in us. But that person is not our model. We have only one model, and that model is no other than our Lord JESUS himself.

This approach has practical value. Suppose you have made Mr. A, or Ms. B your model. Suppose for some reason known or unknown, the said model trips and falls temporarily, or God forbid, permanently: the resultant effect of that is that there will be a chain fall-out effect by all those for whom that individual is the model. If you check 2nd Timothy 4:10, you will find the sad report of a man who went back from following our Lord Jesus. His name was Demas. Suppose he was a model to some young converts: the danger is that they might have gone back with him. That is why JESUS must always remain our model and example, just like the Bible says.

You may be surprised to hear that I had the same problems as a young Christian. I was then in the university as a pre-medical student. The president of the Christian Union Group in the university then was a man that was very humble, so soft-spoken, never upset. Each time I came to fellowship and saw him, I used to get worried. I knew there was just no way I could be like that. He was my model then.

But then, the Lord knew I had that problem. During one of our Sunday afternoon fellowship meetings, one speaker came and said words to this effect: "God does not want you to be like someone else. He just wants to change you." I was noticeably relieved. So you can see that what I am sharing with you now is not original.

Loss of my old friends

Talking about this challenge of staying on course to the end, I am worried that I am beginning to part ways with some of my close friends of old, and I am not making new ones that fast.

That is a natural consequence of being born again; I mean parting ways with some of your good old friends. The way to look at it objectively is to think of the basis of some of those relationships. You may discover that a lot of them are things you will prefer to do without now that you have been born again.

Being born again does not imply that one must break with old friends. Not necessarily. However, what tends to happen is that the moment you start taking definite stands as a Christian, most of your friends will consider you rather dull these days, going on and on about sin, repentance, and the need for salvation. Gradually you will progressively drift apart. But that is not to say that you should not make a concerted effort to keep in touch with them. It is quite likely that God will use you to sow precious seed in their hearts.

What you need to guard against is being dragged back into the old ways through their pressure. From this perspective, you may say that being born again creates a dividing line. It does establish godly, and Holy Spirit inspired, Bible-based living standards, which your erstwhile friends may find unacceptable. I am sure you will share this concern of the Apostle Peter in 2nd Peter chapter 2, from verse 19:

"For a man is a slave to whatever controls him. And when a person has escaped from the world's wicked ways by learning about our Lord and Saviour Jesus

Christ, and then gets tangled up with sin and becomes its slave again, he is worse off than he was before. It would be better if he had never known about Christ at all than to learn of him and then turn his back on the holy commandments given to him.

There is an old saying that "A dog comes back to what he has vomited, and a pig is washed only to come back and wallow in the mud again." That is the way it is with those who turn again to their sin."

- 2nd Peter 2:19-22 [TLB]

The danger you will face moving around as before with your old friends, just as if nothing has happened to you, is the sort of danger that Lot exposed himself to in Sodom while living among the Sodomites.

"And turning the cities of Sodom and Gomorrah into ashes, condemned them to destruction, making them an example to those who afterward will live ungodly; and delivered righteous Lot, who was oppressed with the filthy conduct of the wicked (for that righteous man,

dwelling among them, tormented his righteous soul from day to day by seeing and hearing their lawless deeds)." [2nd Peter 2:6-8 NKJ]

I think you can afford to spare yourself this kind of torment if that is what it means to keep-on with your old friends. God always knows our needs, and I am sure you will soon make new friends who will encourage you in the Lord.

Let us move on to the next thing that will help you stay on course till the end.

Deep Personal Devotion

The other thing that helps a person stay on course without a conscious effort is to develop and cherish a deep personal devotion with the Lord. If one can aim to know God deeply and personally, understand His ways, and strive to follow Him each day, staying on course as a Christian will naturally take care of itself.

Some years ago, I was noticeably worried about this. Two things helped to change the situation for me.

Please tell me what they are

One of them was one of our counselors at the University of Ibadan. An old English gentleman named Pastor S.G. Elton, who has gone on to glory now. It was as if God gave him a mirror into our lives. During one of those group counseling sessions he held for young men and women who wanted to go deeper with the Lord, he had said: *"Let me tell you young men and women,"* he began in his crackling voice. *"Whatever your ambition in life may be, you will never be better than God can make you."*

At the end of that session, he called on us to dedicate our lives totally to God. I responded heartily, convinced in my heart that God and I would be partners together in my life, for my greatest conceivable good. Somehow, it helps young Christians know that deep personal devotion to God can only work to their advantage, contrary to earlier held notions and beliefs. You will remember that we had talked earlier about developing a quiet time habit where we study the Bible and pray. This is a follow-up to that talk on *"Quiet Time,"* the motivation for it, and the depth of commitment we bring to it. These will determine how much progress we make, and how "effortless" the journey will become in time.

Fellowship with other Christians

I believe the person who said that the Christian life might be likened to the experience of mountaineers attempting to scale a peak, hit the nail right on the head when it comes to the need in the life of the Christian, to fellowship with others. Mountaineers are accustomed to supporting each other. If anyone loses a vital foothold, those who have firmer footings at the time, rally to help him or her up.

There is nothing like a Christian who is an island, isolated and aloof from the rest. It is the most potent recipe for a short-lived Christian life.

What we see in the Bible, which is true to experience universally, is that those who seek out the fellowship of other believers serve to strengthen others' faith and be strengthened by their faith.

The apostle Paul put it this way to the Church in Rome:

"For I long to visit you so that I can impart to you the faith that will help your Church grow strong in the Lord. Then, too, I need your help, for I want not only to share my faith with you but to be encouraged by yours: Each of us will be a blessing to the other."

- Romans 1:11, 12 [TLB]

Again in his letter to the Hebrews, he also had this to say:

"Let us not neglect our church meetings, as some people do, but encourage and warn each other, especially now that the day of his coming back again is drawing near." *[Hebrews 10:25 TLB]*

He detailed in his letter to the Corinthian Church, how a person should attend fellowship or Church, and what expectations they should have.

26Well, my brothers and sisters, let's summarize. When you meet together, one will sing, another will teach, another will tell some special revelation God has given, one will speak in tongues, and another will interpret what is said. But everything that is done must strengthen all of you.

27No more than two or three should speak in tongues. They must speak one at a time, and someone must interpret what they say.

²⁸*But if no one is present who can interpret, they must be silent in your church meeting and speak in tongues to God privately.*

²⁹*Let two or three people prophesy, and let the others evaluate what is said.*

³⁰*But if someone is prophesying and another person receives a revelation from the Lord, the one who is speaking must stop.*

³¹ *In this way, all who prophesy will have a turn to speak, one after the other, so that everyone will learn and be encouraged.*

³² *Remember that people who prophesy are in control of their spirit and can take turns.*

³³*For God is not a God of disorder but of peace, as in all the meetings of God's holy people.*

- 1 Corinthians 14:26-33 [NLT2]

I am sure you can see from all these, that when a person attends a fellowship of Christians, he or she goes intending to be blessed and also used by the Lord to bless others.

A person may well say: "I don't think I need any fellowship." That may be true. But he or she certainly cannot say that the fellowship does not need him or her. That is for the fellowship or Church to decide. You may check out 1st Corinthians 12: 12-27 for more information. Here is what verse 27 says:

"Here is what I am trying to say: {i.e. a kind of summary} all of you together are the one body of Christ, and each one of you is a separate and necessary part of it." [LB]

Dependence on the Holy Spirit

We have said quite a few things about this before. All that is left here is to highlight a few more practical details.

I believe that we should lean on the Holy Spirit so heavily that He can almost literally feel our weight. I did not know this at all when I gave my life to Christ. But over the years, I have come to realize that following your Spirit guide in every situation every day, is the surest way to get to the shores of eternity in due course.

When I expressed my concerns about the future, I recall what the Lord said to me one day at the University of Ibadan's chapel gardens. He told me that if I can follow Him each day, one day at a time, then I will follow Him till the end. It has stayed with me ever since. You will notice that this is not new at all. Our Lord Jesus Christ repeated it quite often in His famous statement: "Sufficient unto the day is the evil thereof."

Let us end this by saying that our future is secure in Jesus's hands, provided we are quite willing and quite happy to leave it there.

5.

JUST BEFORE WE PART

I would like to share a few things with you before I leave.

Please go ahead.

The Love of God for You

The first one is the Love of God for you

That would be quite interesting. I have wondered about that in the past. I am glad you mentioned it. Please go on.

Something is quite helpful to know, no matter what the situation in your life may be.

And what may that be, please?

It's probably better to put it in the form of a maxim: "God loves me no matter what."

I am sure you will agree that that needs some explanation. It isn't that obvious all the time. Certainly not!

I do know what you mean, like in difficult and unpleasant circumstances and when things go awry. Yes, I do know. It is at such times more than any other that you need to remind yourself that no matter what is happening in your life and circumstance, you can depend on the love of God to see you through. This approach relies on a few concrete facts about God.

Please go on

- God knows everything that has happened or will happen to you.

- The Love of God will always provide you with a way of escape in every situation.
- God can do whatever He has said in His word anytime.

Now let us look at these a bit more closely. The first one deals with God's Omniscience.

You know that is where I have the problem. If indeed He knows, then why does He let some of these things happen?

It is probably too much for anyone to say they know why things happen, except, of course, they have a revelation from the Lord. But that is not as important as knowing that whatever may happen, you can handle through the Love, Grace, and provisions of Power and Authority in Christ Jesus. This is the faith that turns an adverse situation into a testimony, for adversities often provide the opportunity to demonstrate the love and the power of God at work in us. This is why you must remember that God always provides a way of escape in every situation; however, tempting.

13Every test that you have experienced is the kind that normally comes to people. But God keeps his promise, and he will not allow you to be tested beyond your power to remain firm; at the time you are put to the test, he will give you the strength to endure it, and so provide you with a way out.

- 1 Corinthians 10:13 [TEV]

I believe what the Bible says here is that God expects us not to buckle under pressure but to use the authority He has provided for us in Christ Jesus to correct the adversities in our circumstances. You should check out these references: Ephesians 1:15-23; 3:14-21; Philippians 2:5-11; 4:13; Colossians 2:9,10:

There are many passages to check out, but perhaps we should defer that till another visit.

You should, however, note one of the passages listed above:

"Now glory be to God who by his mighty power at work within us is able to do far more than we would ever dare to ask or even dream of - infinitely beyond our highest prayers, desires, thoughts, or hopes."

- Ephesians 3:20 [TLB]

It is comforting to know that God's power to answer prayers and perform miracles beyond our wildest imagination is already at work within us. It is possible to tap into that power and use it for ourselves and others. You can begin to tap into it now by learning to use the authority in the NAME and the BLOOD of JESUS

Temptation

I would like you to talk a little bit more about temptation. Sincerely, I'd rather not have temptation at all than look for a way of escape.

I suppose what you have said goes for each one of us. The Bible teaches that we can learn how to be victorious in temptation and that there is usually a reward at the end.

"Happy is the man who doesn't give in and do wrong when he is tempted, for afterward, he will get as his reward the crown of life that God has promised those who love him.

And remember, when someone wants to do wrong, it is never God who is tempting him, for God never wants to do wrong and never tempts anyone else to do it. The temptation is the pull of man's own evil thoughts and wishes.

These evil thoughts lead to evil actions and afterward to the death penalty from God."

- James1:12-15 [TLB]

The best time to begin to fight temptation and sin is at the pulling stage. It's no use waiting till you are trapped in it before you can start to look for a way of escape. Once you notice the pull towards evil, begin to rebuke the evil forces in the mighty name of Jesus. Ask the Lord to show you what to do to escape the power of that temptation. Once He shows you what to do, then go right ahead and do it in obedience.

Temptations that won't go away

I need to say a word or two about temptations that won't go away. You seem to see them at every turn and encounter them at every stop. It would help if you recognized that the seed of that temptation is sown in our flesh any time you encounter such pernicious problems. It has somehow become habitual and is ever tripping us up and causing us to fall or fail. In the Book of Hebrews, chapter 12 and verse 1, the Bible calls them besetting sins. Some besetting sins owe their power to our rationalization: like when we say: "I am not the only one; this happens to everybody;

the pressure in the environment is just too much," and such like accommodative statements.

I found help with such sins from the Scripture in Romans 6:7,

7For when we die, we are set free from the power of sin.
- Romans 6:7 [TEV]

This Scripture tells us that we escape the clutches of temptations, particularly those recurrent ones through death. This analogy is meant to reveal that if we can live a deadened life to sin, the attractive power of sin will lose its grip on us.

The Bible teaches that mortification is the way out of temptation.

5You must put to death, then, the earthly desires at work in you, such as sexual immorality, indecency, lust, evil passions, and greed (for greed is a form of idolatry).
- Colossians 3:5[TEV]

But how does one do that? How can one put these evil desires to death? The Bible says the Holy Spirit is the one that does it.

12Therefore, dear brothers and sisters, you have no obligation to do what your sinful nature urges you to do.

13For if you live by its dictates, you will die. But if through the power of the Spirit you put to death the deeds of your sinful nature, you will live.

14For all who are led by the Spirit of God are children of God.

- Romans 8:12-14 [NLT2]

How does the Spirit of God put these evil desires to death for us?

This is the way the Spirit of God works death in us:

First, there must be a sincere desire to stop committing that particular sin.

Secondly, you must put that desire to God in prayer and ask to die to that sin to be free from it.

Thirdly, you must believe that your prayer to be deadened to the attraction of that particular sin has been answered. With that, you begin to confess that you are now dead to that sin and freed from its grip.

Fourthly, it is the confession that triggers the power of the Holy Spirit to deaden the desire.

The testimony always follows. You never can tell how the desire left you, but you know that it has left you. That is the mystery of it.

This is just a parting shot. You may dismiss it in a few sentences on your way out.

What is it? If it is important to you, I will spare the time.

Going to Church

I don't know how you will feel about this, but what do you think about belonging to a church? I haven't been to church in ages, and I think all these churches are the same.

I am glad you asked this question. I remember the late Pastor S.G. Elton giving us an old man's wisdom, had said to us: *"If you ever find a perfect church, do not join it. The moment you do, it will cease to be perfect."* No human organization is perfect, so no one expects the church to be perfect. But when you know that fellowship is two-way traffic, you join a church where you can be fed, and also help to feed others. A church always provides a useful forum for Christian service and Christian growth.

Is there nothing that should guide an individual as to which church to join?

This is the sort of question one must answer with extreme caution, knowing how various denominations protect their membership. But personally, what has always guided me is where the Word of God is taught, and my soul nourished. This sort of forum exists in various denominations. I judge the spiritual food I receive anywhere I go to ensure that they are based strictly on the Word of God and that the teacher is always able to cite his or her authority, book, chapter, and verse. The same also goes for forms and rituals.

This is what has been called the Berean Christians' approach, mentioned earlier (Acts 17:11). They received God's word and searched the Scriptures daily, whether they could find an adequate correlation. Having said this, one must be careful to avoid so-called Christian groups whose rituals smack of spiritism.

Exactly what do you mean by that?

Spiritism involves contact with demon spirits who are under the control of the devil or Lucifer.

The best thing to have is an inquiring mind. Ask questions about practices; are they based on Scripture? What about the prescriptions for special prayers and the like; is there any biblical basis? If there is a genuine doubt, and you suspect that the practices are not in line with God's Word, then the best thing is to opt-out and go somewhere else.

A high index of suspicion is often required. Whenever there is so much emphasis on visions and demonstrations of power with little or no concern for holiness, I believe one must begin to be suspicious. The gift of discernment of spirits, given by the Holy Spirit comes to our aid in this regard. We shall talk about this another time. Always ask the Holy Spirit to guide you in all your decisions. But let me just say that you can never go wrong in a place where there is an emphasis on godly living.

This was the same point the apostle John was making by the Holy Spirit in his letter.

"Oh, dear children, don't let anyone deceive you about this: if you are constantly doing what is good, it is because you are good, even as he is.

But if you keep on sinning, it shows that you belong to Satan, who since he began to sin has kept steadily at it. But the Son of God came to destroy these works of the devil. The person who has been born into God's family does not make a practice of sinning, because now God's life is in him; so he can't keep on sinning, for this new life has been born into him and controls him - he has been born again, so now we can tell who is a child of God and who belongs to satan. Whoever is living a life of sin and doesn't love his brother shows that he is not in God's family."

- 1st John 3:7-10 [TLB]

You may check out 1st John 2:1 and 2 by yourself.

A suitable fellowship of believers for spiritual growth will be a place where people are empowered to do three things:

a. encouraged to give their lives to Christ and be born again;

b. encouraged to pursue holiness with vigour;

c. empowered to develop a deep personal walk with God.

As I said, this exists in several denominations. God is moving into long-established denominations with the same message of the new birth with encouraging results. Vibrant preachers of Gospel truth are emerging in many places to anchor God's move and meet the hunger in the hearts of men for God. Some pastors in very long-established Church groups are now permitting fellowships within their churches that encourage people in this way. Many born again Christians are feeling the call of God to stay in their denominations to work so that others may see the Light of Jesus too.

For a new convert, though, the emphasis is on feeding and spiritual growth. If this is not available where you are, you may find it in a group fellowship that may not necessarily involve changing your Church denomination. You may then go on to your home base to share the things you are learning from God's Word if and where they let you.

The other thing that one should look out for is heresies. You may say that as a new convert, you would have problems here. That may be true. But Jesus did sound a strong note of warning with these words, in Matthew chapter 24:

"Take heed that no one deceives you. For many will come in my name saying I am the Christ and will deceive many. Then many false prophets will rise up and deceive many.

Then if anyone says to you, Look, here is the Christ, or There, do not believe it. For false Christs and false prophets will arise and show great signs and wonders so as to deceive, if possible, even the elect. See, I have told you beforehand. Therefore if they say to you, look He is in the desert! Do not go out, or look, He is in the inner rooms! Do not believe it. For as the lightening comes from the East and flashes to the West, so also will the coming of the Son of man be."

- Matthew 24:4,5,11, 23-27 [NKJV]

As you can see from the above passages, the danger can be averted by a working knowledge of God's word, the Holy Bible. The fact that our Lord Jesus said that even the elect is in danger of being deceived should make us guard our faith jealously against all heresy, and the only way to judge heresy is to measure it against the revealed Word of God in the Bible. Any doctrine that does not measure up to the truth, as stated in God's

Word, deserves only to be dumped in the garbage can where it rightly belongs.

But then as a young convert, I am quite vulnerable.

Only to a limited degree, I will say. God, who has called you out of darkness into His marvelous light, will keep you, [1st Peter 1:5] provided you are determined in your heart to serve Him sincerely. Stories abound of people who were misled for a while. But the love of God found them and opened their eyes to the truth in God's word, and as soon as the truth dawned on them, they changed course.

It does not have to be that way. A prayerful watch, an ardent study of God's word, and constant fellowship with God's people will help a great deal to protect the individual. Most people go into these errors when under pressure or have isolated themselves from the rest of the brethren.

Others do so as a result of a craving for new things. One should always be careful and prayerful. A safe rule is never to let yourself go beyond your depth too fast. You need time to consolidate the many new things and principles you are learning about following God. The Bible cautions us with these words in Ephesians 4:14.

"Then we will no longer be like children, forever changing our minds about what we believe because someone has told us something different, or has cleverly lied to us and made the lie sound like the truth." [TLB]

Part of what is implied here is that the Lord Jesus's various ministry gifts to His Church - Apostles, Prophets, Teachers, Pastors, and Evangelists will be there to steer us all away from error. You may check this out from Ephesians 4: 11 - 16. How to recognize these gifts, and those who have them are subjects for another day.

This has been a wonderful visit. I have really gained a lot. But nevertheless, I should not let you go without asking this question.

If you insist, why not?

I know you said quite a lot about joining a church. I think I agree with you now that it is something a Christian ought to do as part of his or her effort at spiritual development. But you know I am quite worried about some of the things I hear about these churches, particularly those that emphasize that one must be born again.

Precisely what are you worried about?

It is this question of asking people to bring ten percent of their earnings. I doubt that they have any authority in the Bible to do that. It sounds so unfair to collect so much money from people that way. I doubt that I will stay in any church where they teach that.

I am quite happy that you mentioned this. You may be surprised to hear that I felt the same way, too, after giving my life to Christ. Mine was actually for a different reason. I felt that removing ten percent of what I had would create more problems for me. I was an undergraduate at the university then. I felt that I couldn't part with that much.

So what made you change your mind?

That is a long story, and I am not sure you would want to hear it today.

If you can wait to tell it, why not?

Of course, I can wait to tell it.

6.

THE MINIMUM GIFT

I'd like to let you know that I have a personal testimony about what I call the 'minimum gift.' Before I share my testimony, I suppose I need to tell you some of the principles related to giving of one's substance towards the furtherance of the Gospel of the Kingdom of God.

Please go on

One way to look at it is to visualize what it cost our Lord Jesus to bring us our redemption. But please don't get me wrong. I am by no means implying that I saw it all so clearly from the beginning. By the time you have heard my story, you would see why I am careful to mention this, so you do not get discouraged.

Please go on. I cannot wait to hear the whole story.

I recall a tract I saw many years ago on this. It was put pictorially and served to drive the message home. There were ten loaves of bread illustrated. The gentleman kept nine in one heap and held one grudgingly in his hand. The nine loaves had this written over them: FOR SELF. The one loaf in his hand had: FOR GOD written on it. And then below the picture was this: Who could be so mean as to give less?

I believe the letter to the Philippian church detailed what it cost our Lord Jesus Christ to bring down our salvation. That Scripture stated a vital principle that we may summarize in these words: the way up is down. In other words, the path to material progress and prosperity is not to hold on to what you have, but to give away part of it as a seed. The more you give, the more you receive so that you can support the work more. Here is what the Bible says in Philippians chapter two.

"Your attitude should be the same as that of Christ Jesus: Who being in very nature God, did not consider equality with God something to be grasped but made Himself nothing, taking the very nature of a servant, being made in human likeness. And being found in appearance as a man, he humbled himself and became obedient to death - even death on a cross!"

- Philippians 2:5-8[NIV]

You may say that our Lord Jesus was on His descent in these verses. He was God, but for our sakes, He abandoned all the privileges of deity to take on humanity's limitations. Consequent upon that descent, he found that He needed even to go lower and die the death of a criminal to achieve redemption for us. This is a tremendous sacrifice, and the Bible tells us in the book of Hebrews chapter 12, where the inspiration came from:

"Let us fix our eyes on Jesus, the author and perfecter of our faith, who for the joy set before Him, endured the cross, scorning its shame, and sat down at the right hand of the throne of God. Consider Him who endured such opposition from sinful men, so that you will not grow weary and lose heart."

- Hebrews 12:2-3 [NIV]

Our Lord Jesus was very much conscious of the reward of His tremendous sacrifice. We who believe in Him as Saviour and Lord are the rewards of His sacrifice and His joy. Each day as we experience the victory and power that is ours through Christ Jesus, He is pleased with the fruits of His labour.

Now, if an individual has received this Good News of redemption in Christ, it will be naive to imagine that it does not cost money to disseminate. Printing of tracts, translating and printing Bibles, paying the wages of ministers of God, building sanctuaries and places of worship, etc.: All these cost money. Who does God expect to pay these bills but the beneficiaries of the blessing? If the truth in God's word has blessed your life, kept your home, kept you healthy, protected you, prospered your business, etc. Then, paying to disseminate or publicize that truth to benefit others should be your joyful responsibility.

The way you have put it now, one wonders if there is any justification not to pay. But then it does not have to be ten percent strictly. I know some people cannot afford to spare ten percent of their income regularly.

Now that you have mentioned it, I think it is time for me to continue my story.

Yes.

I was actually in need when I stumbled at this truth in God's Word several years ago. I needed to assist my family in supporting my education at the University. I asked the Lord to come to my aid and provide me with alternative sources of income. In our University Christian Fellowship then, there was a need for money. The Fellowship owed money to some university department for services rendered in the previous academic year. They asked us to give up ten percent of our income to meet the need and that God will provide for us according to His promised word in Malachi 3:8-12:

"Will a man rob God? Yet you rob me, But you ask, 'How do we rob you?' In tithes and offerings. You are under a curse - the whole nation of you - because you are robbing me.

Bring the whole tithe into the storehouse, that there may be food in my house, Test me in this way says the

Lord Almighty, and see if I will not throw open the floodgates of heaven and pour out so much blessing that you will not have room enough for it. I will prevent pests from devouring your crops, and the vines in your fields will not cast their fruit," says the Lord Almighty. Then all the nations will call you blessed, for yours will be a delightful land, says the Lord Almighty." [NIV]

The ten percent you are complaining about is really what the Bible calls the tithe. But the Bible also talks about offerings. Therefore, what we are talking about is not just tithe, but tithes and offerings used to promote the Gospel of Jesus Christ, which has now come to mean so much.

After I heard about this, I went to the Lord and promised that I would start giving if I could earn some new money. I told Him that what I had then was not enough for anything. You know, the Lord said something to me that was quite interesting.

When you say the Lord spoke to you, what exactly do you mean?

He spoke to my heart. It was not an audible voice. You get to learn sooner or later how God speaks to you. You see, what you have come into is a relationship, and relationships by nature are two-ways. You talk to the Lord, and the Lord talks back to you. But maybe we should leave that for another time.

O.K. What exactly did He say?

He told me that if I couldn't pay from what I had, there was no guarantee that I would pay from what I will get.

And what did you say to that? Because I think that is true.

I asked the Lord to trust me. That I certainly would pay from the new one. The one at hand was just not enough. He wouldn't say anything after that, and my situation rather than improving deteriorated. Things got worse for me. And if you look at that passage we have just read, you will notice that it says something about preventing pests from eating away what you have.

Anyway, to cut a long story short, I decided to pay when things were not getting better for me. After I gave my tithe, I became like a bird let out of a cage. I spent the rest of my little money buying books and Bible study guides for my students in the Scripture Union groups that I visited. We were called senior friends in those days by these students. Two to three weeks after this, all my money had gone. I remember that day clearly as if it was yesterday.

What did you do? It must have been a desperate moment.

You bet it was. I recall that I knelt by my bed that morning and said a prayer that is somewhat like this: "LORD if this thing is working, then it had better work now. You can see that my money is completely finished". It wasn't a long prayer at all.

And what happened?

It was like fiction, almost incredible. Long before that, I had written a radio play. I had been to the station several times, but the producer kept telling me that he had not had time to look at my work. So after numerous fruitless trips that drained whatever little money I had, I gave up. But that morning when I got to the lecture theatre, that producer was there by our anatomy lecture theatre. He was not looking for me. He had come to see someone else. But then he saw me and called me, and told me that he had used one of my plays and that I had six pounds and six shillings to collect. You could have knocked me down with a feather.

I bet one could have indeed. Interesting, very interesting indeed.

You will now understand why I believe very strongly that giving your money or time or talent to support the work of the Gospel of Jesus Christ is doing yourself a favour. Because if you give cheerfully with the understanding and burden that someone else should hear this Gospel that has done so much good in your life, then God will ensure that you have enough and to spare so you can continue to give.

The Bible puts it this way:

"Remember this: Whoever sows sparingly will also reap sparingly, and whoever sows generously will also reap generously.

Each man should give what he has decided in his heart to give, not reluctantly or under compulsion, for God loves a cheerful giver. And God is able to make all grace abound to you, so that in all things at all times, having all that you need, you will abound in every good work.

Now he who supplies seed to the sower and bread for food will also supply and increase your store of seed and will enlarge the harvest of your righteousness.

You will be made rich in every way so that you can be generous on every occasion, and through us your generosity will result in thanksgiving to God.

This service you perform is not only supplying the needs of God's people but is also overflowing in many expressions of thanks to God.

Because of the service by which you have proved yourselves, men will praise God for the obedience that accompanies your confession of the Gospel of Christ, and for your generosity in sharing with them and with everyone else.

And in their prayers for you their hearts will go out to you, because of the surpassing grace God has given you."

- 2nd Corinthians. 9:6-8, 10-14 [NIV]

I have always believed in contributing my widow's mite.

I hope you recognize what that means?

It means the little you can afford.

No, not really, that is not what it means. I think we should look at the passage and see what it says:

"Jesus sat down opposite the place where the offerings were put and watched the crowd putting their money into the temple treasury. Many rich people threw in large amounts. But a poor widow came in and put in two very small copper coins, worth only a fraction of a penny. Calling his disciples to him, Jesus said, "I tell you the truth, this poor widow has put more into the treasury than all the others.

They all gave out of their wealth; but she, out of her poverty, put in everything - all she had to live on."

- Mark 12:41-44 [NIV]

So you can see that the widow's mite isn't giving the tithe or ten percent, but one hundred percent. It took me quite some time to realize this. I used to think like you that the widow's mite meant the little you can afford. It means all that you have in your storehouse or bank account. Maybe you need to think twice about the widow's mite after today.

I can tell you it will not be easy.

Nobody says it is easy. But after you have started, I am sure you will be able to say like David in Psalm 34 verse 8: "Oh taste and see that the Lord is good. Blessed is the man that trusts in Him."

You know, part of the problem I will have is the lifestyle of some of these preachers. That will worry me.

Why should that worry you? Is it because they are preachers?

Not really, but I think they should live moderately to encourage those who give. You don't want to feel that all you are doing is making them live in luxury.

I think the best way to look at this is to know who you are giving your money. When you sow a seed for the Gospel's furtherance, you are not giving the money to the preacher; you are giving it to God. God will bless and prosper you for giving to Him and His work. If the preacher happens to misuse it, he or she will answer for that before the Lord. I will give you a few examples.

In the Old Testament of the Bible, you will find that God made adequate provision to care for His servants. You may check this out in Leviticus 2:1-3, 10; and 10: 12-15, as well as Malachi 3:8-12.

But some abused it, and if you check the records, you will see that God punished them for it. One example is the sons of Eli in 1st Samuel 2:12-17. You need to see what verse 17 says:

"This sin of the young men was very great in the Lord's sight, for they were treating the Lord's offering with contempt."

You may check out the rest of that judgment in 1st Samuel 3:11-14.

I hope some of these guys have seen these Scriptures you are referring to.

It is not our place to stand in judgment of anyone. God is the judge of us all. I always try to remember that. It was David who said: "If you regard iniquity Oh God, who will stand." But that is not to say that ministers as custodians of God's people's offering to the Lord, towards the extension of His Kingdom, do not have a responsibility to walk in integrity and accountability. They do, and this is the way the apostle Paul put it:

"I am sending another well-known brother with him, [i.e. referring to-Titus] who is highly praised as a

preacher of the Good News in all the churches. In fact, this man was elected by the churches to travel with me to take the gift [i.e. referring to their offering] to Jerusalem. This will glorify the Lord and show our eagerness to help each other. By travelling together, we will guard against any suspicion, for we are anxious that no one should find fault with the way we are handling this large gift. God knows we are honest, but I want everyone else to know it too.

That is why we have made this arrangement.

- 2nd Corinthians 8:18-21 [LB]

I do not doubt in my mind that most ministers of the Full Gospel of our Lord Jesus Christ are quite conscious of the great responsibility they owe the body of Christ to walk in conscience and integrity before the Lord in every area. This is the way the apostle Paul put it.

"We try to live in such a way that no one will ever be offended or kept back from finding the Lord by the way we act so that no one can find fault with us and blame

it on the Lord. In fact, in everything we do, we try to show that we are true ministers of God." [2nd Corinthians 6:3-4TLB]

Well, well, well. I could say I am reasonably convinced. I pray that God will help me to start this immediately. But tell me how He will return what I have given.

I doubt that anyone can say that with any precision. But that He will return it in multiples, is something even I can guarantee on His behalf, after many years of walking in this way. He always returns in abundance, far greater than you gave. The Bible puts it this way:

"Give, and it shall be given unto you; good measure, pressed down, and shaken together, and running over, shall men give into your bosom. For with the same measure that you mete withal it shall be measured to you again"

- Luke 6:38 [KJV]

I learned firsthand what the Bible meant by the phrase, *"shall men give into your bosom."*

What happened?

I had just bought a new car and wanted to take out comprehensive insurance on it. My insurance agent told me that I had lost my No Claims Bonus, which should reduce my premium by 50%. I got to church the next Sunday, and the Lord asked me to give a particular amount of money as an offering. I did. When I went to my agent subsequently, hoping to pay another installment towards my premium, I was pleasantly surprised to hear that my bonus had been re-instated by the insurance company. What I had paid so far had covered my insurance premium. So really, no one can say how God will return a gift by a cheerful giver. But what I can say for sure is that He always does.

I must say that this has been wonderful, quite an eye-opener. I have enjoyed it.

I am glad you have. But let me say this besides. After you have started giving towards the extension of the Kingdom of God here on earth, you will discover that tithing as good as it is, is simply a kind of schoolmaster, to train us to start to give. The idea behind the widow's giving, which we just talked about, is more consistent with the New Testament teaching on giving.

I hope you are not implying that we should give all we have away?

Not really. But the principle is that Christ was willing to give all He had away for us. God demanded it of Him, so He had to give it. The example He has laid for us is that we too must learn to be willing to give all that we have for the extension of the Kingdom for which Jesus came and died. Once we are willing, then whatever fraction of it that God demands of us, I say, God, not the preacher, we shall give. The Apostle Paul admonished that everyone should give as they have purposed in their hearts. In essence, what that means is giving as the Holy Spirit of God has directed no matter how persuasive or unpersuasive the preacher may be.

I can see that we need to take time to discuss how one can hear from God. That will assist us in giving what God wants us to give when He wants us to give it, and where He wants us to give it for the extension of the Kingdom of God in the hearts of men and women.

You are certainly right there. God will then be able through us all, to distribute the resources available, to areas where there are needs, to avoid waste in the worldwide family of God.

That will be something like Divine Economic Planning.

More like Divine Budgeting if you please.

I can bet you we are still quite far from there.

Not really. As more and more individuals learn to hear from and obey the Holy Spirit's voice in their lives, then like a jig-saw, assembled piece by piece, the whole will gradually emerge.

We all pray so,

7.

THE ASSURANCE OF SALVATION

But just before I leave, I would like to ask you my parting question.

What is the question?

You may pardon my asking it: but are you truly born again?

I certainly am, and I mean every word of it.

What makes you so certain about that?

I don't know for sure, but I know I am born again. I feel it within me and have felt it ever

since that very day that I gave my life to Jesus Christ. It has been most exciting I can tell you.

What times do you feel it most?

Oh, times like this, when I am meditating on God's Word and sharing with other people. I feel that assurance within me.

That is very lovely, indeed. I am glad that you do feel it. The Bible says in Romans 8:16 that the Spirit of God bears witness with our spirit that we are children of God. That is wonderful, indeed. Every child of God does get to feel that he or she is born again sooner or later.

But you know, being born again is not about the way you and I feel. If it were, then it will vanish the day we do not feel it anymore. It is important to remember that the assurance of your salvation depends entirely on the promise of God. You can rely absolutely on what God has said in His Word.

This is because GOD DOES NOT CHANGE. He said in Malachi 3:6; "*I am the Lord I change not.*"

If God said that if you surrendered your heart to Jesus, you would be born again, then that must settle the matter. It does not matter what I, the devil, nor anybody for that matter, feel about it. It does not even matter whether you feel saved or not. As I said, you eventually get to feel saved, and I am glad that you do. But that is like the "icing on the cake." It is not the cake itself. Your salvation is rested firmly on the promise of God in His word that: 'If thou shalt confess with thy mouth the Lord Jesus, and shall believe in thine heart that God raised Him from the dead, thou shalt be saved.' You may check this out again in Romans 10:9. It is always good to remember that, and let the devil know that you know for sure on what your salvation is based.

I am glad you mentioned this because the other day, I didn't feel that saved.

Why?

Somebody upset me very badly, and I really "blew my top." After that, I didn't feel that saved anymore until this evening when you came, and we started this fellowship.

That is the point I am making. If you do anything wrong after you have been born again and the Spirit of God within you points it out to you, all you need to do is to repent and ask the Lord for His forgiveness. Sometimes, there may be the need to make restitution as the Spirit of the Lord directs, as we mentioned earlier. But that has nothing to do with the covenant relationship that you have made with your God in Christ Jesus. The Bible puts it this way:

"But if we are living in the light of God's presence, just like Christ does, then we have wonderful fellowship and

joy with each other, and the blood of Jesus, His Son, cleanses us from every sin.

If we say that we have no sin, we are only fooling ourselves, and refusing to accept the truth

But if we confess our sins to Him, He can be depended on to forgive us and cleanse us from every wrong. [And it is perfectly proper for God to do this for us because Christ died to wash away our sins.]

If we claim we have not sinned, we are lying and calling God a liar, for He says we have sinned.

My little children, I am telling you this so that you will stay away from sin. But if you sin, there is Someone to plead for you before the Father. His name is Jesus Christ, the one who is all that is good and who pleases God completely."

1st John 1:7-10, 2:1-2 [TLB]

A born again Christian can be 'overtaken' in a fault like the Bible says in Galatians 6:1. The implication is that he or she has not planned to sin, but was unfortunately scuttled by the devil. This is what the Bible means where it says:

"The person who has been born into God's family does not make a practice of sinning, because now God's life is in him; so he can't keep on sinning, for this new life has been born into him and controls him - he has been born again."

- 1st John 3:10 [LB]

The Bible recommends that the fellow be restored to his or her faith by other brethren so that they can return to fellowship with God and man. You may check out Galatians 6:1-5. But this in no way undermines his or her salvation, provided of course that he or she is willing to repent and return to the Lord, striving after perfection and holiness.

Wow! I am sure glad you mentioned this. It's comforting to know. You've been quite helpful.

We must thank the Lord for that. Let us share a word of prayer.

"Heavenly Father, we thank You for Your grace and for Your Holy Spirit, which has taught us today. We come to You to say that we love You and that by Your grace, we shall stay Yours until our lives' end. We know You will do anything and everything to ensure this. By Your grace, we shall cooperate with You and obey You all the way. Thank You for loving us so much, in Jesus name we pray. Amen."

Now just before I step out, let me take one look at my checklist to be sure I have covered everything. Hmmm! I think there is one more important thing I need to leave with you from my checklist.

And what could that be?

Our calling is to be disciples of Jesus. We follow Him. And the purpose of following Him is to be conformed into His image, ostensibly to be like Him.

Really! Is such a thing possible?

Well, the Holy Spirit is our helper in the process. But that is a cardinal purpose of the Father in heaven for sending our Lord Jesus to us. From the beginning, the Father wanted all of us who follow our Lord Jesus Christ to be like Him.

Wow! Where do you find such a purpose stated that clearly?

Ok! Let's take a quick look.

29For those whom He foreknew [of whom He was aware and loved beforehand], He also destined from the beginning [foreordaining them] to be molded into the image of His Son [and share His likeness inwardly], that He might become the firstborn among many brethren.

- Romans 8:29 (AMP)

To be like Jesus? I bet that is a dream.

And to make the dream a reality, our Lord Jesus left His main thoughts in the Bible in what we generally call, THE SERMON ON THE MOUNT. The most detailed version of it is in the Gospel of Matthew chapters 5 – 7. The Sermon on the Mount is a reference for every follower or disciple of our Lord Jesus.

I see

And for starters, our Lord stated the Beatitudes at the beginning of that teaching. The Beatitudes is like an overhauling kit to rebuild us into individuals as close to the original as possible. We all come to Christ messed up in several ways, particularly in our attitude to God and man. The Beatitudes are to straighten us out and put us on a new launch pad that will take us on the right road to our Father in heaven. You may call them our *Spiritual Overhauling Kit*.

Wow! That sounds awesome

Indeed, it does, but I can't start that right now. But here is what I will do. I will send you a synopsis to start you off.

That is a great idea.

ADDENDUM
SPIRITUAL OVERHAULING KIT

Matthew 5:3-12 [NIV]

3"*Blessed are the poor in spirit, for theirs is the kingdom of heaven.*

4*Blessed are those who mourn, for they will be comforted.*

5*Blessed are the meek, for they will inherit the earth.*

6*Blessed are those who hunger and thirst for righteousness, for they will be filled.*

7*Blessed are the merciful, for they will be shown mercy.*

8*Blessed are the pure in heart, for they will see God.*

9*Blessed are the peacemakers, for they will be called sons of God.*

[10]*Blessed are those who are persecuted because of righteousness, for theirs is the kingdom of heaven.*

[11]*"Blessed are you when people insult you, persecute you and falsely say all kinds of evil against you because of me.*

[12]*Rejoice and be glad, because great is your reward in heaven, for in the same way they persecuted the prophets who were before you.*

We should note that for seven out of the eight Beatitudes, there are two parts. The first is the requirement and the second is the reward. We should follow this approach to appreciate each of them.

Blessed are the poor in spirit

The requirement here is poverty of the spirit. The poor in spirit are those who know that outside of the grace and mercy of God revealed through the forgiveness and pardon we receive through the sacrifice of Christ; they have no hope of going to heaven. They know that there is no room for self-righteousness. Our Lord Jesus further confirmed this when He said in the Gospel of John:

"I am the way, the truth, and the life. No one comes to the Father except through Me.

- John 14:6 [NKJV]

King David earlier stated that a broken and a contrite heart is what God needs from us to pardon us from all our sins.

For You do not desire sacrifice, or else I would give it; You do not delight in burnt offering. The sacrifices of God are a broken spirit, A broken and a contrite heart-- These, O God, You will not despise.

- Psalm 51:16-17 [NKJV]

Also, when we have poverty of the spirit, we let God have His way in our lives in all things. The reward of the poor in spirit is the Kingdom of heaven. This is because they do not seek to enter by merit but by grace and mercy. After they have entered, they do the will of God and let God have His way in their lives by choice. The assurance of the Kingdom of God belongs to them because they trust in the mercy of God and do His will on earth.

Blessed are those who mourn.

The requirement in this is primarily those who mourn for their sins. They are those who do not sin with impunity. Instead, any time they do something wrong, they are grieved in their heart that they have made God unhappy.

For the kind of sorrow God wants us to experience leads us away from sin and results in salvation. There's no regret for that kind of sorrow. But worldly sorrow, which lacks repentance, results in spiritual death.

- 2 Corinthians 7:10 [NLT2]

Have mercy upon me, O God, According to Your lovingkindness; According to the multitude of Your tender mercies, Blot out my transgressions. Wash me thoroughly from my iniquity, And cleanse me from my sin. For I acknowledge my transgressions, And my sin is always before me. Against You, You only, have I sinned, And done this evil in Your sight-- That You may be found just when You speak, And blameless when You judge.

- Psalm 51:1-4 [NKJV]

The comfort they receive is God's pardon and the inner strength to conquer their failings. There is also the joy of sins forgiven, which frees them from the burden of guilt from their past. And this guilt can be debilitating in some cases.

Blessed are the meek

The meek are those who carry their strengths with humility. They use their power and ability to serve others not to oppress them.

Come unto me, all ye that labour and are heavy laden, and I will give you rest. Take my yoke upon you, and learn of me; for I am meek and lowly in heart: and ye shall find rest unto your souls.

- *Matthew 11:28-29 [KJV]*

(Now the man Moses *was* very meek, above all the men which *were* upon the face of the earth.)

- *Numbers 12:3 [KJV]*

The reward of the meek is that they inherit the earth. This speaks to the favour they receive from God and man to prosper and increase them in their lives.

Blessed are those who hunger and thirst for righteousness

This Beatitude tells us to go beyond grieving for our sins to strongly desire to get it right all the time before God and man. It also speaks to a driving desire to see righteousness prevail in our world.

For I say unto you, That except your righteousness shall exceed the righteousness of the scribes and Pharisees, ye shall in no case enter into the kingdom of heaven.

- Matthew 5:20 [KJV]

And there he went into a cave, and spent the night in that place; and behold, the word of the LORD came to him, and He said to him, "What are you doing here, Elijah?" So he said, "I have been very zealous for the LORD God of hosts; for the children of Israel have forsaken Your covenant, torn down Your altars, and killed Your prophets with the sword. I alone am left, and they seek to take my life."

- 1 Kings 19:9-10 [NKJV]

The reward is the release of the inner strength to live godly on this earth. This inner strength comes from the Holy Spirit who empowers us and also orchestrates changes in our world as we persevere.

Blessed are the merciful

This Beatitude implies that mercy is a seed, which we sow to reap a harvest of mercy in life. Those who sow mercy in their relationship with others are going to reap mercy in due course.

No mercy will be shown to those who show no mercy to others. Mercy triumphs over judgment.

- James 2:13 [GW]

"Then his master sent for him and said to him, 'You evil servant! I canceled your entire debt because you begged me. Shouldn't you have treated the other servant as mercifully as I treated you?' "His master was so angry that he handed him over to the torturers until he would repay everything that he owed. That is what my Father in heaven will do to you if each of you does not sincerely forgive other believers."

- Matthew 18:32-35 [GW]

Blessed are the pure in heart

The pursuit of inner purity is the primary task for anyone seeking a close relationship with God. It is a compatibility call. Our God is light, and in Him, there is no darkness at all. He is calling us to pursue inner purity in our lives. To see God is to commune with Him in our hearts and sense Him in our lives and be with Him in eternity.

5 God said (to Moses), "Don't come any closer! Take off your sandals because this place where you are standing is holy ground.

- Exodus 3:5 [GW]

But because the God who called you is holy, you must be holy in every aspect of your life. Scripture says, "Be holy because I am holy."

- 1 Peter 1:15-16 [GW]

Blessed are the peacemakers

We are called to lead a life of peace and to be God's agents of peace in the world around us. Our Lord Jesus Christ came to bring peace between God and man and between man and his neighbour.

Suddenly, a large army of angels appeared with the angel. They were praising God by saying, "Glory to God in the highest heaven, and on earth peace to those who have his goodwill!"

- Luke 2:13-14 [GW]

Whenever you go into a house, greet the family right away with the words, 'May there be peace in this house.' If a peaceful person lives there, your greeting will be accepted. But if that's not the case, your greeting will be rejected.

- Luke 10:5-6 [GW]

Blessed are those persecuted for righteousness

When we suffer persecution for being in the right and doing the right, we confirm that we are faithful followers of our Lord Jesus Christ, who work righteousness on the earth. Our calling in Christ is to stand for the Kingdom of God and its righteousness on the earth. The persecution we suffer, serve to confirm our citizenship of the Kingdom of God in heaven.

But let none of you suffer as a murderer, a thief, an evildoer, or as a busybody in other people's matters. Yet if anyone suffers as a Christian, let him not be ashamed, but let him glorify God in this matter.

- 1 Peter 4:15-16 [NKJV]

But even if you should suffer for righteousness' sake, you are blessed. "And do not be afraid of their threats, nor be troubled."

- 1Peter 3:14 [NKJV]

THE END

www.ingramcontent.com/pod-product-compliance
Lightning Source LLC
Chambersburg PA
CBHW060013050426
42448CB00012B/2735